Developing The Ministerial Mindset:
A GLOBAL VIEW

Developing The Ministerial Mindset:
A GLOBAL VIEW

Aliar Hossain & Mark T Jones

authorHOUSE®

AuthorHouse™
1663 Liberty Drive
Bloomington, IN 47403
www.authorhouse.com
Phone: 1-800-839-8640

Published by AuthorHouse   04/29/2013

ISBN: 978-1-4817-8993-6 (sc)
ISBN: 978-1-4817-8995-0 (e)

Table of Contents

Dedication

This book is dedicated to my late uncle Afzal Hossain, who dedicated his entire life to social work and the politics of growth in Bangladesh. He campaigned tirelessly for the emergence of a new politics and urged all major political parties and key leaders to embrace the winds of change. The politics of a country has a profound impact on its levels of development and he encouraged me to undertake further research on the politics of development within the complex scenario of developing nations.Mark and I would also like to dedicate this book to all of those people who have lost their lives or have been victims of political unrest and corruption in developing nations.

Foreword

Professor John Drew—Professor of European Business and Management, European Business School; Director, Institute of Contemporary European Studies

You do not need to have an MBA to run a successful business, but it does no harm. You do not have to have management qualifications to run a successful government department, but it will do you no harm to have some.

Politics is about getting into power and then carrying out successful activities to help you stay in power. This book does not help you to get into power. But its advice on how future ministers could be helped to develop the necessary skills to do their job better is well worth considering. A global standard, let us call it provisionally a Masters in Ministerial Responsibility (MMR), is worth considering.

In the meantime Aliar indicates with examples, how the lack of training for the job can restrict the performance of many politicians when they arrive in power and find they have to manage and deliver, both being abilities which can be challenging and worrying. You are not allowed to drive a car or fly a plane without training—people's lives are at stake. Yet as a minister, millions of people's livelihoods, safety or well-being are also at stake. On the job training may be too little, too late.

This book identifies the need for ministerial training and outlines the advice, methods and subjects which such training might include. Heads of universities and schools, directors of hospitals and charities, government officials and union leaders, all have increasingly to receive appropriate training on their way to high office. Why should the highest offices of a country be the preserve of those whose experience and capability to hold them is at best variable and in some cases leads to unhappy personal experiences and inefficient government?

The author, Aliar shows the need and the ways a start could be made to improve the situation. The means are readily available through the internet, distance learning and the thousands of courses and university degrees currently available across the world which could readily be adapted to help improve ministerial performance in our rapidly globalising society and our interconnected nations.

Professor Abdul H. Chowdhury—Dean of Business School, North South University

In today's world, politicians must prepare themselves to assume a remarkable task, to face the global, social, political, and economic development challenges of the 21st Century. Are they prepared, in terms of education and experience, to undertake the ministerial responsibilities and to deliver the services expected form them? Do they have proper qualifications or training to run a government office successfully? Should they need institutional learning before assuming such positions? Or should they depend on on-the-job training to improve ministerial performance with the nation's majority interest at stake? Answers to all these questions are discussed elaborately in the book titled 'Developing the Ministerial Mindset: A Global View' written by two eminent authors, Mr. Aliar Hossain and Mark T. Jones.

Ministerial training and the professional development of ministers, as well as politicians who intend to become ministers, are an integral part of good governance. Politicians need to change the traditional mindset of governance by extending their attitudes towards cooperation for good causes, considering public opinion and respecting the inner characteristics of the public and its culture.

The most distinctive feature of this book is the incorporation of geopolitical issues and context in the global perspective covering Asia, Europe, Africa and the United States. The first author emphasizes how the current global environment and nation states are heavily dependent on decisions made by ministers, with the evidence drawn from Asian countries as well as from Europe and the United States of America. The second author endeavours to focus on the African context. This book maps the contemporary issues of legislative structures and identifies the need for the professional development of ministerial candidates through formal or informal learning methods. This book has also focused on the discussion of the ministerial administrative issues by contrasting the administrative environment in developed and under-developed nations.

Ministers, politicians, policy makers, administrators, researchers, students, and many other professionals are likely to extract an optimum level of benefit by using this timely presented book.

Mihir Bose—BBC Editor, Broadcaster & International Author

The surprising thing about 'Developing the Ministerial Mindset: A Global View' is not that it has now been written, but that a book like this has never existed before. It deals with the fascinating and very important idea: why do politicians often prove to be such incompetent managers.

We expect politicians to tell us what they will do when they come to office and once they are elected we expect them to fulfil those promises. And, as often happens, when these politicians fail to keep their promises we throw them out. These failures nourish the belief that politicians are all dishonest and they never have any intention of keeping their word. Yet even the most honourable politicians, who have every intention of keeping their promises, have to implement their policies. And is it not unrealistic to expect them to do so when many of them have no managerial experience whatsoever?

There was a time when politicians sought office after they had proved themselves in commerce or other professional walks of life. Half a century ago, most politicians in the British House of Commons had either served in the Armed Forces or had some experience of management in the wider world outside. So while the British wartime coalition saw Labour politicians become ministers with no previous experience of political office, many of them had accumulated vast management experience. The classic example of this was Ernest Bevin who had been a successful leader of the trade union movement and proved an exceptionally successful wartime minister and later Foreign Secretary.

But now not only do politicians, even in the west, come to office with no previous ministerial experience, but many of them have no experience outside of politics at all. Thus for instance, as this book notes, in the current Danish Government of twenty-three ministers, seven have not had a real job since they finished their education. And only a dozen ministers have over five years of work experience of any kind.

It is important to emphasise that lack of ministerial experience may not be a barrier to success. When Labour swept to power in 1945, while some ministers had wartime experience, the man who proved to be the most successful and left behind the greatest legacy of the 1945 government had none. Aneurin Bevan had spent the war criticising Winston Churchill's handling of it, so much so that Churchill had called him a squalid nuisance. Yet appointed Health minister Bevan proved a tremendous success and, in the teeth of opposition from the country's medical profession, he created the National Health Service, one of Britain's most prized possessions.

But since then such achievements have became rarer and politicians have struggled to implement their ideas. This was particularly the case with Tony Blair who, like Bevan, came to office never having held any sort of ministerial appointment. Then despite all the power he had as Prime Minister he found it difficult to implement many of his policies.

In Part One, Aliar Hossain quotes extensively from ministers who confess they found the ministerial experience baffling and the time it took for them to learn things. He also draws an important distinction between politics in the developed world and the developing world, where family ties and corruption still form such an important part of the political scene, further alienating the politicians from the people.

The classic case of this is India. The country, the world's largest democracy, can be proud of the fact that despite being a developing economy it has consistently maintained the democratic structure established after its independence from Britain. Unlike nearly all other former colonies, including the ones in South America, the army has stayed in the barracks and the ballot box has always been the instrument for a change of power. This was true even in the 70s when Mrs Indira Gandhi's emergency rule made Indians aware of what dictatorial rule was like. Yet Mrs Gandhi was removed through the ballot box not tanks.

However the Congress Party which won freedom is now a family party where successive generations of the Gandhi family come to power almost as if it is their royal prerogative. Political families have not been unknown in the west, and still exist in the US, but the way it works in India, and other developing countries such as India's neighbours Pakistan and Bangladesh, suggest the way to power is not programs or any claim to competence, let alone managerial experience, but a family name.

Hossain's answer to all this is a body set up under United Nations auspices to create what he calls a ministerial mindset. The novelty of the idea cannot be denied but it is hopelessly idealistic and I cannot see any politician willing to limit his power in this way.

Part Two by Mark Jones starts out with the proposition that ministers are tightrope artists and suggests ideas for how they might gain more experience of balancing themselves while in office. The author gives many instances of failure. But what is surprising is, in the example of Trinidad where the present prime minister is castigated, no mention is made of the fact that the man who might succeed him, Jack Warner, had to resign from FIFA, world football's governing body, as a result of the corruption crisis in the organisation. Warner's story is an interesting example of the marriage of modern politics and sport particularly in the developing world. A fuller analysis of the case might have yielded more practical solutions as to how politicians can be made to balance better on the tightrope and not fall off as they try to fulfil their declared mission of serving the people.

But for all the somewhat idealistic tone of this book it raises important issues that have not always been highlighted.

Dr Eric C K Chan (Executive Coach & Programme Director, Regent's University London)

As things stand, many ministers in governments across the world are seen as doing little more than simply fulfilling their duties via ticking boxes once having been elected or put into office. In many cases voters receive only empty promises. Most individuals who put themselves forward for these life-changing ministerial positions are ill prepared to take up such postings and to carry out the changes required for the good of their nation.

Notable global ministers who have done well in the past often have good personal value systems and focused vision. These individuals usually have a strong self-belief mindset, which involves a sense of compassion, rapport, duty of care, accountability, knowledge, skills, oratorical presence and resoluteness. They ensure that red tape is kept to a minimum and that they are able to deal with risk management and also to lead.

According to Aliar and Mark, sadly many politicians who take on such ministerial postings lack some of the above key qualities and are badly prepared to take office.

Aliar provides examples of global stories relating to the shortcomings of ministers' capabilities and competencies. He suggests that there is now a need for some sort of finishing school and academy focusing on providing ministerial training and development including coaching, guidance and mentoring. This may be an ideal way forward, but it remains a challenge for would-be ministers to enroll and complete their training prior to taking up their posts. Some may enroll, but they may not be elected.

Mark focuses on the African continent and draws upon his experiences, sharing his view that a successful politician needs to be like a tightrope walker, i.e. to have ambition, application, conviction, courage, judgement, mental and physical agility, as well as nerves of steel.

This book is a good starting point in developing an effective ministerial mindset and capabilities for politicians for the future by reflecting on the practices of today.

Acknowledgements

I would like to offer my special gratitude to Professor John Drew for his foreword and for offering his specialist knowledge and expertise in reviewing this book. His incisive and pertinent advice has been a source of intellectual nourishment throughout this endeavour and has contributed to shaping the argument that stands before you.

I am indebted to Professor Abdul Moyeen (Former Minister, Bangladesh), Professor Hannan Chowdhury (Business Dean, North South University), Dr Eric C K Chan (Executive Coach and Programme Director, Regent's University London) and Mihir Bose (BBC Editor, Broadcaster & International Author) for their contributions to his work. It is my fortune to have benefited from their timely advice, given with the grace and clarity for which every author would wish. Their engaging comments have gone to the heart of the matter and of this book, and their shared sentiments regarding the status quo have been a source of support.

I would also like to thank my friend Danny Winkler for assisting me during the review period. There are many who have helped to contribute to this book in a myriad of ways who go unnamed. The thoughts presented here are the culmination of thought, logic and observation which no individual formulates alone. The book is the better for the consideration, the time and the opinions of many whom I have come across in my professional life.

Finally, I am beholden to my family who furnish me with the joy and desire to seek to improve the world for the future. This book could not have been completed without the continued support of my wife and the many untold kindnesses that enable me to devote my time to this issue.

Target Audience and Why

There is a growing awareness beginning to emerge in certain parts of the world as regards the competencies of government ministers and the pressing need that something could be done. The successes and failures of those in power have been a source of concern and analysis since time immemorial, so why now?

The world stands at a challenging and exciting time—globalisation ensures a greater competition of ideas and over resources, while transparency is ever more accessible. The corporate world has taken the lead in promoting training for those in management, so that it is almost inconceivable that those at the helm of major companies and non-governmental organisations have not been fully briefed and prepared for the roles they have assumed. This leaves ministers in a unique position of taking on responsibilities for which they have had no training, and what is worse, for which they have no prior knowledge or even a conception as to what they might entail.

This book is therefore aimed firstly for those who have a professional involvement and interest in this field—politicians, civil servants, policy makers, academics, commentators, advocacy groups, and educational trainers in all regions of the globe. It outlines the need and scope for the introduction of new mechanisms that will address the status quo and provide for a more sensible arrangement in the preparation of government ministers. But as the book suggests—what is needed is not only a new approach to training government ministers, but mechanisms to promote a ministerial mindset characterised by duty, integrity, capability and responsiveness.

As such, the target audience for this book is all those concerned with civil society and the implementation of policies—whether concerning the environment or sustainable business development, from the richest country to the poorest. In the world of global competition and the emergence of alternate forms of governance, no country can assume that the established mechanisms will not be overtaken by new methods elsewhere in the world, or that their way of doing things is sufficient.

The world is changing, and this book is written for those who seek to ensure governance keeps pace with these transformations, rather than lag behind, with the consequent damage to the prospects and health of the people and the environments which are governed.

PART 1

Developing the Ministerial Mindset: A Global View

By Aliar Hossain

<u>Preface</u>

The change that new ministers experience is immediate, one that is occasionally unexpected or for which they are unprepared, and it requires a radical transformation in their workload, responsibilities and in the nature of their interaction with others. It is, in short, an uncompromising and sudden jolt to their lives. Tiernan and Weller describe how the realities of government soon temper the satisfaction of achieving office.

> "Ministers must tackle a range of issues, often brutal in their complexity. They know that, whatever they do, some groups in the country will be unhappy with the result. They know there is no single answer. Indeed, often it is hard to get agreement on what the issue actually is." Alongside with the daily routines of managing their political duties and personal lives, it requires "ways of managing time, information, access and expertise, if ministers are to have any chance of meeting those diverse expectations."[1]

At the heart of this book lies the intention to increase ministerial capacity, responsibility and judgement, through formal processes of training that will enable ministers to claim a greater grasp on the subject of their department and the techniques necessary to implement this knowledge.

As such ministerial training encompasses two broad aspects—firstly the issues and knowledge necessary for overseeing the sector-specific responsibilities of a minister's department and, secondly, the skills required to successfully lead and manage a government department.

Introduction

> If I ever describe the process of becoming a minister—moving from one ministerial job to another—to somebody in almost any other job outside they think it is, frankly, pretty dysfunctional in the way that it works. That's not just this government . . . I think we should have been better trained. I think there should be more induction. There's more now than when I started as a minister but it's still not enough. I think there should be more emphasis given to supporting ministers more generally in terms of developing the skills needed to lead big departments, for example. When I became Home Secretary, I'd never run a major organisation. I hope I did a good job but if I did it was more by luck than by any kind of development of those skills.
>
> Former UK Home Secretary Jacqui Smith[2]

The job of minister is one of the few senior positions for which there exists little or no systemised mechanisms of support for new appointees. While the idealised, and not necessarily inaccurate view, of politicians as inspired individuals lends a natural reluctance towards training, the emphasis of a formal training process is not to diminish individual initiative or maverick tendencies. Such a process would run counter to the intentions and motivations of the politicians and electorate themselves.

Furthermore, the intention of training is not to build successful ministers *per se*—this is a much larger task that involves a multitude of concerns regarding selection, pre-appointment preparation (which should take place over the course of several weeks), a long-term programme of skills development, and continued monitoring and performance review. Kenneth Clarke, the highly experienced UK government minister, has observed, "By the end of two years you are beginning to understand what you are doing."[3] The aim of training is to get ministers up to speed to a *satisfactory* level. This may sound at first glance a limited goal, but it is one that in many countries around the world governments and the civil service are *failing* to meet. The proposition is clearly to give ministers the tools, support and knowledge they need to enable a smooth transition to departmental duties and to enable them to carry out the programmes they wish to implement.

Overcoming Inertia

The question is, what can and should be done to assist newly appointed ministers to cope and perform at their highest level. Given the hectic schedules of ministers—who have to juggle ministerial, political, constituency and personal responsibilities—what set of procedures will support and not further encumber ministers in effectively pursuing their agendas, which have an incalculable impact on the lives of millions of people.

One of the barriers to instituting formal introductory training procedures is the natural reluctance that comes from unfamiliarity with new ideas, despite such processes being universally instituted across the senior echelons of the corporate management world. This can be further exacerbated by the nature of political life, where to acknowledge weakness or inexperience can be considered by some to be detrimental to one's perception by others, thus seemingly harming one's career aspirations. It is natural that politicians, whose rise has been due to a measure of power—whether through power bases or support from those in power—will be reluctant to fully engage in this process to begin with. However, putting in place a set of systemised training processes will enable this to quickly become a routine and welcomed aspect of ministerial accession. Secondly, the universal implementation of it will reduce egotistical reluctance from individuals. By nurturing a lineage of knowledge engagement with predecessors, it has the side benefit of encouraging a greater openness to listening to the viewpoints and assessments of others, a valuable attribute for ministers in roles and departments in which they may have had little experience or exposure.

The Importance of Negotiating the Early Days

> "I do not recall ever being given any indication of what was
> expected of me on being appointed to any political job."
> Former UK Minister Michael Heseltine[4]

The importance of stressing the above is not to give an impression that the role of a minister is an impossible one. It is one that suits those who have a natural flair for the role and for those for whom timing and circumstance are propitious. The value of training is in preparing ministers for the crucial initial period upon which success or otherwise is often determined.

The reason for the importance of the initial phase is twofold:

1. Firstly, relationships and positions forged early on will colour relationships over the course of an appointment—whether this be with industry partners or internal civil service employees. A minister must understand what style of government is most effective—an issue that has emerged into the spotlight over the last fifteen years. Whether business is conducted through established civil service structures, reformed 'sofa government', through the influx of personal advisors, or through the contracting out of civil service advice to private bodies—this sets not only the tone of the administration, but potentially affects the conduct and efficacy of departmental work, can affect the nature of advice proffered, impinge on the comprehension of the consequences of actions, and alter the balance of responsibilities.

   Furthermore, initial positions taken in respect of those whom the department has policy responsibility over—whether this be welfare or business—will affect future relationships and, in the case of certain policies, the support necessary for their successful evolution and implementation.

   A government department, by the nature of its size and the many groups and individuals affected by its policies, is a large ship that takes considerable time to manoeuvre and change course. This is further exacerbated by the almost instant nature of response and coverage provided by the media and affected groups on social networking mediums.

2. The second reason for the importance of this initial phase in a ministerial appointment is the long lead-in period necessary

for the successful completion of policy. Initially, research and analytical preparation is necessary to accurately ascertain current and past conditions and policies. A new policy must be devised, alongside contributions from selected partners and experts, followed by a lengthy consultation process. Subsequently a policy must be prepared for legislation and pass through the parliamentary system. Once successfully passed into law, and assuming it has not been irretrievably altered in the process, it awaits implementation—a process requiring organisational adjustment and the establishment of new networks of civil service and external partnerships to enable its effective dissemination into the wider economy and society. From this point onwards, and depending on the nature of the policy in question, there will be a lag period only after which it will be possible to ascertain the success or otherwise of the policy and to have an opportunity to make adjustments. The length of this process is variable, however it often extends beyond the lifetime of many a departmental minister and in some cases beyond the administration of many a government—hence the critical importance, given an impatient populous, to act quickly. The pressures facing a minister to get up and running, often before the minister is fully in control of all the requisite facts, are therefore immense and an established process of training will enable the accumulated benefit of hindsight and knowledge to provide assistance during this critical phase.

What does a formalised training process entail?

A consistent theme emerging from interviews conducted with former ministers in the United Kingdom is their admission of having felt under-prepared for taking office, and for the tasks and challenges ahead. The situation is no different on the other side of the world:

> There are courses for almost every occupation, but there is no course that teaches you how to be a member of parliament, and there's no course that teaches you how to be a minister. It's assumed that if you are elected, you can be an effective minister. There is no training course and, unless you ask, no one volunteers to help.
>
> An anonymous former Australian Minister[5]

The proposition is not to set a qualification for becoming a minister. Ministers are political appointments and should remain so. Many of the skills necessary to becoming a successful minister are the same for those in other professions—sound judgement, people and communication skills, leadership and team working aptitudes, managerial capabilities, time management and so forth. The task of ministerial training is to provide specific support: introducing a new minister to the tasks, scenarios and structures of the ministerial workplace, and providing instruction in sector-specific knowledge relevant to the department. It is apparent that a far more encompassing and strategically designed process is required, beyond the poorly thought-out and ad-hoc support that exists and varies from country-to-country and government department-to-department globally, which can contribute an element of certainty and grounding to an often chaotic and extemporized set of circumstances.

Training encompasses areas such as strategy, policy and delivery. It reflects an acknowledgement that political leadership and government is an art with which one, given natural abilities, can be trained and equipped to carry out. While not a guarantor of success, it offers the best hope for improvement in performance and effectiveness.

There are several aspects to training:

1. Defining objectives
2. Assistance in leading (or for junior ministers, working within) a government department
3. Supporting ministers for the assignment's accompanying challenges
4. Understanding the departmental brief
5. The concept of global development

1. Defining Objectives

> It's very important and difficult not to be distracted from your long-term strategic objectives by tactical opportunities which may come your way.
>
> Former UK Home Secretary Michael Howard[6]

An essential and proven aspect in ministerial success is displaying confidence in the direction of policy, even if at the outset this may yet remain unformulated. Managing a government department can often appear not too dissimilar to the experience of sailing a small boat through a large ocean storm. Swells approach with rapidity, some unforeseen, waves roll over the bows, the boat is battered from all directions and there appears nobody from the outside able and present to extricate one from the situation. Tossed and turned, it takes strength of character and an ability to see beyond the present storms, to keep attention focused on the destination ahead. The minister knows all to well that failure to navigate these choppy waters and to effectively handle subordinates under one's charge will result in him or her being forced unceremoniously to walk the plank.

In this manner, how helpful is a chart and descriptions of the final destination, supplied from those who have already made the journey? And so we should ask ourselves, why is there not in place a formal process of introduction and training informed by past experiences to enable new and inexperienced ministers to perform ably and forearmed with a degree of comprehension as to the experiences that lie ahead?

One of the most important factors in ministerial effectiveness, as rated by ministers and senior civil servants in the United Kingdom, is possessing a clarity of vision and of objectives.[7] A successful approach to ministerial duties involves defining objectives, thereby setting out a clear plan ahead that can remain visible when the fog of politics falls, characterised by competing interests and short-term pressures. While this may be supposed to be highly dependent on the character of the minister, one of the elements of training is to provide a clear picture of what life as a minister is like and what strategies can enhance effectiveness. One of the priorities of ministerial training is to assist ministers being cognisant of ways to reduce distractions and deviations from long-term strategy placed on them by relentless demands in the pressurised environment. Of specific relevance with regard to the emotive issues characterising policy debate, maintaining due diligence and established mechanisms and protocols can assist in sustaining a long-term balance that helps to override destabilising situations. Preparing ministers for the importance of defining clear goals, and enabling a forward vision of the likely paths of policies, strategies and circumstances, will better steel them for negotiating the difficult waters that lie ahead—whether in terms of managing the minutiae or in dealing with unfavourable events.

2. Leading a Government Department

Another clear objective of training is to give ministers a clear appreciation of the departmental structure they have inherited and the roles and responsibilities incorporated within it. Understanding where management, direction, responsibility, authorisation, analysis, assessment and other such functions lie within the department will enable more trust to develop between an incoming minister and civil servants. Past evidence strongly points to an insufficient level of trust in this relationship, often sparked by uncertainty as to the support structures and capacities existing within a government department, as being a repeated cause of departmental discontent and failure.

One of the benefits for a minister that can be derived from trust within this relationship is the benefit of shared knowledge provided by accumulated civil service expertise. The UK House of Commons Public Administration Select Committee has noted, "the civil service can give a long-term perspective which may not be available to ministers. However, it will only be able to perform this function if its members are respected and trusted."[8] There exist many examples of mistrust leading to poor decision-making and assessment of facts, though few bear the depth of consequences of the UK Labour Government's refutation of intelligence gathering and Foreign Office opinion in the determination of the Iraqi security threat under Saddam Hussein prior to the Second Gulf War.

> "I had no idea of what was involved. I had to learn to be a minister, moving from decision to decision, seeing how they get made. I had no managerial training."
>
> One anonymous former UK Minister of State[9]

Mutually identifying the limits (under normal circumstances) of ministerial department intervention is significant in generating trust and in allowing ministers and civil servants to focus on their roles within the department to the maximum of their abilities. As one senior UK civil servant stressed, "The main thing we've got to do is to convince them that we are competent—they ask us to do something, we deliver it."[10] While such is the standard for professional relationships, it is important to bear in mind that the bear pit of politics is a confrontational environment, where those not in power spend a proportion of their time criticising the performance and implementation of existing policy, while any natural reluctance towards teamwork is accentuated in surroundings where rivals exist all around. In short, trust requires the devolving of responsibility and avoidance of the temptation to micro-manage. While it can be hard for a minister to relinquish managerial control, given that it is the minister who often bears responsibility for collective failure, providing an introduction to the full scope of responsibilities and workload facing a minister will enable clear and immediate decisions for how a minister will intend to allocate his or her valuable time and energy. In the instance that a minister's intention is the improvement of managerial performance and delivery, a focus on micro-management is an essential component, and training will help in providing initial guidance on past performance and the framework in which this has been conducted.

3. Supporting ministers for the assignment's accompanying challenges (e.g. time management and communications)

Increased media assertiveness and access further adds to the necessity for tighter rules of ministerial conduct. Every word is scrutinised, every meeting is questioned, every silence is pondered. It is unrealistic to expect new ministers—surrounded by a whirlwind of new pressures, colleagues and concerns—to further be able to master all these tasks. Training will enable a measure of independence in judgement, acquisition of key skills and knowledge, and the critical self-assurance that comes from the initial provision of support. The admissions of many ex-ministers reveal their desire to be supported in their new task—to demystify their role and responsibilities and to gain a measure of understanding that will place them in good stead when confronted by the countless faces seeking their time, answers and direction.

> I went from being the opposition spokesperson with a staff of two where your only responsibility was really to get into media, and maybe develop some policies, to supposedly being minister and having notionally more than 60,000 employees working under you. And there is not nearly enough training.
>
> Jackson (pseudonym), former minister,
> state level, Australia[11]

Ministers oversee large organisations and work within a hierarchical framework of policy implementation that extends far beyond the civil service itself to other parliamentary bodies and to the participation of private organisations and individuals. One of the necessities for effectively turning ideas to policy to legislation and then to implementation is therefore to ensure wide support and goodwill.

Issues such as time management and communications strategy are two of the critical areas here in which training is able to lay down clear guidelines to ease the day-to-day burdens on a government minister. These also offer clear examples of the long-term benefits that can accrue from short-term and simple, but effective strategic training and support.

4. Understanding the Departmental Brief

Government ministers are responsible for vast budgets and coordinating national legislation affecting business interests, citizens and the economic and social well being of the nation. As well as the imperative to determine the general direction of policy, ministers are required to oversee and to comprehend the complexity of minutiae that, in highly specialised and professional environments, often determine the success or otherwise of government policies.

Few occupations require more immediate hands-on engagement and capacity to preside over an array of tasks and subjects, as do ministerial appointments. Ministers are required to assess existing strategies, evaluate methods of managing partnerships with political and other relevant bodies, set in place an effective communications strategy to publicly answer questions on policy matters, determine the direction of government policy and its priorities, rapidly initiate long-term research towards these aims (accompanied by associated electoral and political time pressures), and prepare strategies for turning policy into legislation. Some of these complex responsibilities may lie further down the line, however missteps in the critical early phase can derail longer-term strategies, and so it requires ministers to be on the ball from the start—in relation both to action or discussion.

Yet, ministers are often elevated to positions and departments for which they have little past experience or affinity, and lack an in-depth knowledge that will enable them to plot the correct steps ahead. This requires an understanding of the history of prior interventions, efforts, successes and failures.

Ministers also benefit from an independent knowledge that will enable an accurate assessment of advice and contributions from interested parties. While some of this can be delegated to civil servants, there remains the need for ministers to take strong decisions and take responsibility for them.

Furthermore, the increasing privatisation of advice and services traditionally conducted by publicly paid civil servants, now undertaken by special advisors and corporations (such as private accountancy and consultancy firms) has increased the scope for those with vested interests—either directly or indirectly—to influence the decision-making and policy-making processes. The number of political advisors has increased rapidly in many countries, in the case of the United Kingdom doubling over the course of the Labour administrations from 1997 to 2010. Emboldened by the growing ethos of privatisation, governments have sought to assist ministers in the increasing complexity of their work by increasing the number of supporting advisors and staff. However, by dissipating ministerial responsibility, there remain questions as to a possible reduction in ministerial authority and capabilities, necessitating ministers to maintain a strong hold over their brief.

This paper acknowledges the increasing complexity and workload faced by government ministers and approves of the support of trained and experienced civil service staff and of alternative viewpoints that can be gained from other valuable advisors. Nevertheless, by contrast to the recent rapid growth of special advisors, ministerial training will give greater capability directly to the hands of ministers themselves.

<u>Supporting Ministerial Longevity</u>

While politics is characterised by unpredictability, tumultuous events and responses, and the due concern to mitigate short-term issues, there remains considerable scope to improve the area of ministerial succession planning and training. Indeed, with greater succession planning comes the possibility for improved ministerial training and the ability to remove some of the instability, uncertainty and reflexive decision-making that currently takes place. Furthermore, ensuring time and effort has been devoted to helping ministers learn the specific and general skills required may increase stability of appointments and continuity in policy, where currently the continual flux in ministerial personnel and direction in certain countries reduces policy effectiveness and civil service enthusiasm for engaging fully with agendas that might change in future months.

One of the biggest obstacles to the success of ministerial performance and of long-term policy is the frequency of government reshuffles. Ostensibly to reward ministers and politicians who have adequately carried out the tasks assigned to them, the practice often calls into question the importance placed upon sector-specific specialisation. While the practice reflects the capacity of individuals to master a multitude of subjects and rewarding excellence, the frequency of reshuffles and the standard absence of long-term coordinated strategy surrounding them, signifies a less attentive attitude towards the importance these decisions have for government performance and the sectors under their oversight.

Reshuffles, particularly when wide-ranging and implemented suddenly, reduce the scope for long-term succession planning and for politicians to prepare for their forthcoming briefs. Events such as the emergency June 2012 reshuffle of five ministers in the Japanese cabinet by Prime Minister Yoshihiko Noda in an effort to win opposition support for a bill designed to double sales tax, indicates that short-term pressures little to do with the competence of the ministers themselves can play a determining factor in ministerial assignments. Moreover, the exigencies or conflicts within politics often lead to appointments by political favour, as with the March 2012 sacking of the highly regarded Najob Balala, Kenyan Minister for Tourism, in favour of an inexperienced successor.

In these instances, the government machine would be well served by an established and comprehensive mechanism to enable new ministerial appointees to develop the necessary skills amidst these tumultuous events. The adoption of a standardised mechanism seen as part and parcel of the appointments process would allow for the flexible and responsive meeting of the needs of the new minister.

Ministerial profiles

The pool of talent from which to select ministers varies from country to country. Many are restricted to members of the legislature, including United Kingdom, Canada and Australia. However, other nations have a freer hand in ministerial selection, including the United States, Germany and France, where candidates can come from the world of business, academia, the non-governmental sector and elsewhere. This enables the direct infusion of talent and skills of those who have recent and firsthand experience of the sector to which they are being appointed, and of the direct effects of previous government policy in this regard. While this has obvious attractions, it also opens the possibility for an interested party to assert undue influence with potential issues for conflicts of interest, as in the case of the appointment of former Goldman Sachs CEO Henry Paulson, Jr. to United States Secretary of the Treasury. Furthermore, any inherent bias or change in working environment, as suggested in the transfer from the business or academic environment to government, would benefit from a process of orientation provided by a systemised training programme.

For most ministers assuming office, this is the first time they have had the opportunity to manage large departments with multiple outcome responsibilities. Many have come from small entrepreneurial backgrounds or worked their way up the rungs as career politicians. However, the position of minister encompasses roles and responsibilities that they are unlikely to have combined previously: that of political advocate, parliamentarian, departmental manager, public face and communicator of an organisation, theoretician, problem-solver, diplomat and negotiator. This list, which yet does not cover all aspects of the ministerial position, illustrates this unique role and the necessity for preparing new appointees. The former Chief Executive of oil multinational BP and UK government minister Lord Simon of Highbury, "compared effectiveness in leading a department to conducting an orchestra, being able to conduct different instruments, the strings of the civil service and the brass of the politicians".[12] Preparation in this respect refers to preparing ministers for the scope of all eventualities, the responsibility and support framework, the accumulated experiences of predecessors and the network of communications and relations to be negotiated. And this has not yet even begun to touch upon the departmental-specific knowledge necessary for effectively determining policy and strategy.

Ministerial profiles in the developing world

The determination of the pool of potential ministers is affected by the specific conditions in each country and therefore cannot be assumed to be similar worldwide. The conditions that affect this pool include the nature of civil society, spread of education, standards of wealth, human rights, security, corruption, social attitudes, cultural norms and historical precedent.[1] For developing countries such as Bangladesh, Nigeria, the Philippines and Columbia, the construction of a local power base offers a strategic foundation for political success, in a manner that is rarely exhibited in developed nations. In the latter, this emerges as a consequence of more developed and integrated national systems of power. It also affects the nature of, for want of a better categorisation, personal fiefdoms. In developed nations these are more likely to be absorbed within established political and corporate frameworks, requiring an increased focus on the tools necessary to succeed. The character of localised fiefdoms in developing nations requires a stronger emphasis on additional tools, including money, local control and power. These tools are required and exhibited in the developed world, but carry less weight. As such, a successful power broker-politician in the developing world is more likely to display the successful attributes associated with building a power base. The difficulty, as has been described above, is that such qualities are not necessarily those that will serve democratic, meritocratic, effective, non-clientialist ministerial decision-making.

At the same time, there exist many educated and successful professional individuals who have entered politics to contribute their experience and particular knowledge. The question is whether

---

[1]   This issue cannot be dissociated from that of electoral finance. In order to shed further light on the subject, we will later discuss patterns and developments in electoral finance globally.

the governmental system in developing countries is sufficiently embedded, extended and absorbed in a nation's culture and practise. What makes a political system function, apart from the power structures and socio-economic conditions existing at a particular moment, is the social memory, an intuitive accepted mode of practice upon which individuals and society function. It is, in part, a sub-conscious routine supported by social rewards and penalties. In developed countries, where national political structures have emerged from a combination of bottom-up and top-down evolutions that have been negotiated in compromise through centuries-old adjustments, this is likely to be far more embedded than in developing countries, where top-down structures alien to traditional power structures have had barely a few decades to come to reconciliation.

As such, it becomes increasingly important for ministers in developing countries, governing in this milieu, to be strongly equipped with the support of training to assist them in their tasks, given that they are less likely to receive strong support from political mechanisms and more likely to face clashing systemic structures, than their counterparts in the developed world.

Global development

Political leaders across the world have built up a reputation for breaking promises and lying to their local constituents and the international public. If this is to be corrected, it can only be achieved through greater education and training of ministers, providing a greater understanding of their roles, responsibilities, scope for action, support mechanisms and the processes of formulating policy and overseeing governmental departments. How is a minister to deliver on promises without the experience, understanding or full attributes to do so? In this, ministers are blind as to the processes involved in delivering promises. It is the job of ministerial training to correct some of these deficiencies.

In this, a global perspective is of increasing importance. As nation states increasingly become absorbed within a global political village or cross-border agreements, integration and consensus, it is mandatory that global political leaders understand it and act accordingly. It is also necessary that ministerial training incorporates this global development. It requires a set of minimum global standards and acceptable practices, supported through globally recognised training that not only maintains standards across nations, but enables better interchange and dialogue between them. In this, it is important not only for a minister in Pakistan to be trained to, and display, the same standards as in Finland, but to be able to understand the practices of the other. By comprehending the methods of ministerial interaction, the actions of each will be more easily comprehensible, smoothing the path for better cooperation.

Current practice concerning ministerial training in the developed world

Informal training and support takes places in the developed world, with civil service bodies usually providing this function. Over recent years, there has been growing awareness of the value of training, however there exists no globally recognised process and initiatives remain in their infancy. The international record is patchy. Some administrations opt for brief informal sessions, while in the US and New Zealand written guidance has in the past been placed at the disposal of new ministers.[13]

In the United Kingdom, the National School of Government briefly ran a ministerial programme, however this school has subsequently closed. In the last few years the Institute for Government has begun to offer discreet training for government ministers, while Oxford University has opened the Blavatnik School of Government to prepare future political leaders. The United Kingdom currently spends $1,500 training each minister—a small sum compared to the billions of dollars for which they are responsible.

> "On 2 May 1997, I walked into Downing Street as PM for the first time. I had never held office, not even as the most junior of junior ministers. It was my first and only job in government."
>
> Former UK Prime Minister Tony Blair[14]

In the United Kingdom, preparation for government by political parties exists on a makeshift basis, with a few sessions for shadow Labour Party ministers having taken place prior to their winning the 1997 election, and similarly for senior Conservative politicians in the run up to forming a coalition government with the Liberal Democrats in 2010 (although their Liberal counterparts forewent such limited preparation).[15] The Conservatives' process elicited more success, which can be seen as a benefit of accrued experience, however its successes fall far short of those that would be targeted by a systemised training process.

> I do not think stigma is the problem. I think the problem is the lack of a culture being inculcated from the top, encouraging and indeed requiring ministers to take part in appropriate training events. Secondly, it is the timetable to which most ministers work, where pressures are enormous and it is very easy to commit yourself in advance to something and then on the day to say, "I really cannot justify this because there are so many other pressing requirements of time".
>
> Former UK junior minister (1997-2005)
> Nick Raynsford[16]

Despite repeated efforts by UK ministers to propose, and in some cases initiate, training sessions, the result has been a poor take-up by colleagues, often due to the optional nature of such sessions within a busy workload, exacerbated by its anomalous character within a culture that does not prioritise skills development from the top.[17] An essential aspect of formal training lies therefore not only in its character and design, but in its implementation across the board with strong institutional emphasis placed upon it as a mandatory element of ministerial accession.

A vision for the developing world

It is envisaged that in the developing world a comprehensive approach should be taken to enable ministers to reach a minimum standard of competency, knowledge, skill and awareness necessary as the first step to efficiently taking on ministerial responsibilities. This training must be immediate but flexible, on a short-term ongoing basis that accommodates the calls on the minister's time, and through a step-by-step methodology enable the minister to come to grips with assignments in unfamiliar policy areas and at a hitherto untested professional level.

Ministerial training in practice

In order to ensure global best practice it is necessary to construct a training and discussion forum that accommodates the range of relevant experience—from local to global.

Sessions should be developed in specific stages addressing key considerations for new ministers. These will be constructed on a country-by-country basis in order to ensure relevance to local conditions and circumstance, however they will be informed by globally accepted practice.

In so doing, it is necessary to establish a central advisory body with the experience learned from a wide range of countries and first-person experience, acknowledging the latest studies and surveys from the field. Establishing rigorous procedures and training areas will ensure universal coverage of the issues as detailed above, allied with a flexibility to design training programmes to meet particular needs and timings.

The benefits of a unified body will accrue in the on-going knowledge and lessons learned during the training sessions, helping to further improve the suitability of the training process in later years. To be clear, we are starting from a low level of existing training practice and knowledge diffusion. To achieve the goals outlined in this booklet requires a strong and consistent engagement, with the vision to accomplish long-term change in the way the political system and ministers engage with each other.

Electoral finance

Electoral funding provides an insight into the nature of political systems. It helps to define the scope of democracy, the loci of power and legislative procedures in a country. If the vast amounts sometimes spent by individuals and groups in an election appear to be a poor use of funds, it must be remembered that donors, valuing this precious resource, expect something in return. As was the case in the Watergate scandal of 1976, the phrase 'follow the money' is never more apt, for by following the trail one can identify how and where it flows. While it is easy to view funding negatively, the essential criteria should always be the use to which it is put. Here we analyse funding in three countries and look at alternative international models, providing a snapshot of the global picture and trends that lie within.

USA

Each time national Presidential or Congressional elections loom, an accompanying side-story describes the record levels of election funding involved. This is no less the case than in the 2012 campaigns, which according to the Center for Responsive Politics will have cost an estimated $5.8 billion, up 7% from the $5.4 billion spent in 2008. Prising the two elections apart, the race for the Presidency will have cost in the region of $2.5 billion, slightly down on the $2.9 billion spent in 2008, while the Congressional elections will have seen a rise in spending from the $2.5 billion of the 2008 election to an estimated $3.3 billion.

Federal funding regulations regarding Presidential elections in the United States permit several channels of funding:

1. **Individual donations to Presidential campaign teams.**
   These are recognised as either small ($200 or less) or large ($200 plus).

2. **Direct party funding**
   This is raised independently over the course of election cycles.

3. **Political Action Committees (PACs)**
   PACs were designed to circumvent legislation aimed at preventing the influence of corporate or union funding on federal elections. Coalescing under the 1971 Federal Election Campaign Act, corporations and unions were able only to organise and administer PACs, accepting a maximum of $5,000 in contributions from individuals. There

are currently 4,600 active PACs, able to direct their funds into candidates' or party coffers. Disclosure of donors is required in 38 states, however reporting is permitted on either a monthly or quarterly basis, enabling avoidance of disclosure in some cases until after the relevant elections.

4. **Corporate or union donations to Presidential campaign teams (Super PACs)**

This has been the major change affecting funding regulations in recent years. In 2010 the Supreme Court ruled that it was now permissible for corporations and unions to make direct donations to influence federal election campaigns, although the prohibition on their directly funding candidates and parties remains. As a consequence, these organisations are able to use their own funds to subsidise independent electioneering campaigns on behalf of a candidate, party or issue with the proviso there is no coordination between them. Leading contributors to the Presidential campaign of Mitt Romney include Goldman Sachs, JPMorgan Chase, Morgan Stanley, Bank of America and Credit Suisse, while leading contributors to Barack Obama include the universities of California and Harvard, Microsoft and Google.

5. **Social welfare groups**

These are also known as 501(c)(4) organisations or not-for-profit organisations. Importantly, as electoral funding is not considered to be the primary purpose of such organisations, they are not required to disclose their funding sources. Not-for-profit organisations are allowed to influence political agendas as a form of public welfare, primarily through independent advertising campaigns. The benefits of this channel revolve predominantly around the scope for tax-exempt status for donations, the lack of individual limits and the ability to maintain privacy. In view of their tax-exempt status for charitable purposes, social welfare groups have faced increasing controversy, especially as television advertising spending by this group exceeds that of the Super PACs and all other independent sources.

As a guide to the relative value of each source of funding, the donations received as of September 2012 for both the incumbent Democratic candidate Barack Obama and the Republican nominee Mitt Romney are shown.

Figure 1: Donations received by Barack Obama and Mitt Romney campaign teams for the 2012 US Presidential election, as of September 2012

Source	Democrats	Republicans
Individual donations ($200 or less) To: Presidential campaign teams	$137 million	$37 million
Individual donations (above $200) To: Presidential campaign teams	$213 million	£156 million
Funds raised by the parties' National Committees	$210 million	$239 million
Super PACs	$25 million	$89 million

An ongoing trend, and one that is increasingly global, is the move away from spending related to individual events and rallies towards media campaigns in the forms of advertisements and online communications. Industry analysts Needham and Company have estimated total 2012 campaign spending on TV networks at $5 billion, an increase of nearly 80% on the £2.8 billion spent in 2008. Providing such a large income stream, this also presents potential issues regarding reporting, particularly given US networks' dependence on advertising revenue.

United Kingdom

To compare the difference in scale in electoral funding, the general election held in the United Kingdom in 2010 cost participating parties a total of $49 million—equating to a spend per head of population of $0.80 compared to $19 per capita in the United States. While both derive from Anglo-Saxon models of democracy, their implementation and structures are very different, exhibited in the nature of elections and electioneering. While the US system has traditionally sought to place a ceiling on contributions, the United Kingdom has adopted an approach to limit electoral spending while enabling unlimited individual contributions.

Figure 2: Campaign costs over recent UK general elections:

Election year	Number of Constituencies	Number of Candidates	Total Long Campaign Spend[2]	Total Short Campaign Spend[3]	Total Expenditure	Average Spend Reported Per Candidate
1997	659	3,724		12,929,207	12,929,207	3,472
2001	659	3,319		11,885,785	11,885,785	3,561
2005	646	3,554		14,171,960	14,171,960	3,988
2010	650	4,150	11,298,207	14,065,542	25,363,749	3,489

Strict limits exist on the expenditure of individual candidates, with a base ceiling of £25,000 during the long campaign and £7,500 during the short campaign, plus an additional 5p per borough/burgh (urban) constituent and 7p per county (rural) constituent.

---

[2] The long campaign spend refers to the period before electioneering took place proper, from 1 January 2010 until the dissolution of Parliament on 12 April 2010.

[3] The short campaign spend refers the election campaign from the dissolution of Parliament until the day of the election.

Electoral parties also face a limit on spending, which in the 2010 election stood at £19.5 million. This represents a significant departure from the US model, magnified since the Supreme Court's decision to allow unlimited contributions and the emergence of the Super PACs. Yet no single UK party reached the legislated limit, with the Conservative Party spending £16.7 million compared to £8 million by the incumbent Labour Party and £4.8 million by the Liberal Democrats. In the last three months of 2009 the Conservative Party raised £10 million over a quarterly period for only the second time in its history. Compared with the £2 million it received during the equivalent period in the run-up to the 2005 election, it illustrates how party finance in the United Kingdom is especially influenced by the perceived likelihood of victory. Interestingly, the Labour spend reflected a drop of £10 million from the previous campaign indicating the scope for downward trends, and indeed this shortfall was not fully absorbed by the other parties. In the 2010 general election, the 43 political parties contesting seats spent £31.5 million between them, down from the £42.3 million spent in 2005.

Although parties receive a small level of state funding, primarily to support certain administrative costs, they rely almost completely on donations, which enable the parties to support themselves throughout the electoral term as well as building electioneering war chests. Donations tend to rise in the run-up to an election and between 6 April and 6 May 2010, the month before electoral polls were held, the UK Electoral Commission registered that the Conservative Party received £7,317,602, Labour received £5,283,199 and the Liberal Democrats received £724,000. Transparency is strictly monitored, with national parties required to declare all donations above £5,000 and local party associations required to declare donations above £1,000. The Conservative Party is most dependent on corporate backers, while the Labour Party remains heavily reliant on funding from the trades unions.

India

While not an issue that has gained national attention in the United States, there have been discussions in the United Kingdom and India regarding state funding of political parties to contest elections. Behind this proposition is the desire for electoral reform and to remove private finance and its influence from politics. The concept of privileged interests has provided for a problematic debate—as witnessed in the United Kingdom with considerations of influence by corporate backers on the Conservative Party and trades unions on the Labour Party. This proposition is summarised by West Bengal CM Mamata Banerjee, writing, "Without economic freedom, political freedom is not complete".

Historically, unlimited corporate funding was a part of early independence party funding, however in the late 1960's, corporate donations in India were proscribed. Nonetheless, the loss of this income flow was not balanced through alternative sources, such as state contributions, resulting in continued, but now hidden, corporate contributions. The loss of transparency and legality resulted in a more heavily *quid pro quo* system of rewards, reflecting the importance to democracy of transparency in contributions. Since 1985, corporate donations were once again legalised and from 2003 made tax-deductible, with disclosure necessary for all contributions above Rs 20,000. Nonetheless, the change in the law has not resulted in increased open donations, a factor of shifting party politics and the fear of adverse consequences of ending up on the losing side. In 2008-2009, Rs 201 million of the Rs 480 million received by the Congress Party, and Rs 1,652 million of the Rs 1,960 million received by the Bharatiya Janata Party, came from donations below Rs 20,000, thus avoiding disclosure and scrutiny.

The Association for Democratic Reforms and National Election Watch have calculated that political parties in India have earned

Rs 4,662 crore since 2004 through a combination of donations and other sources. The primary recipients over this period have been the Congress Party with Rs 2,008 crore and RJP with Rs 994 crore. However this masks a wide variance in the composition of income flows, with donations comprising 14.5% of Congress income compared with 81.5% of RJP income.

In 2011, the electoral expenditure limits for candidates were raised, continuing a process of increasing the artificially low ceilings set during the 1990's. The limits for each candidate now stand at Rs 40 lakh for parliamentary constituencies and Rs 10 lakh for Assembly seats. However the failure of full disclosure by candidates, political parties and local associations increases the difficulty of adequately confirming election expenditure. In the February 2009 Lok Sabha elections, total candidates' expenses were recorded at Rs 11.2 billion, but with additional party expenditure and informal spending by associates, the figure was predicted to be two or three times this amount. While candidates' spending is limited, others are legally allowed to fund unrestricted campaigns on their behalf. The upcoming 2014 Lok Sabha elections are predicted to costs in the region of Rs 100 billion, a reflection of the increased economic stakes in a rapidly emerging economy.

Alternative models have emerged, with the concept of electoral trusts led by the Tatas and other corporate conglomerates, 36 of whom existed at the time of the 2009 elections, contributing over Rs 1 crore to political parties. In the case of the Tatas, this provides support to independent candidates during an election campaign, but not beyond this limited term.

International Alternatives

Such a model is also reflected in German state financing (accounting for around 25-30% of total funding) for political parties whose electoral support reaches above a certain threshold. Half the funds are delivered prior to an election campaign with the other half transferred after the poll date. However in Germany it has been debated whether over-reliance on state finance has been detrimental to democracy and to political responsiveness to the popular will, and a renewed emphasis has been placed on increasing small and corporate donations, allied to tax-deductible status.

Nonetheless, Scandinavian countries lead the way in public funding for political parties in an effort to reduce corruption and the influence of 'big money' on elections and politics. In 2010, state-derived funding accounted for 74% of the income of political parties in Norway.

Returning to the US experience, an experiment in election financing has existed in New York City since 1998, called the Small Donor Matching Funds programme. An optional scheme to which most candidates have opted in, over time this matching scheme has reduced the size of allowable individual contributions and risen the multiple of fund-matching, thereby increasingly prioritising the smallest contributions. It now provides state top up on a 6:1 ratio of all verifiable small donations for up to $175 received by each participating candidate, whereby an original contribution of $175 results in an overall value to the candidate of $1,225. This is intended to reduce the influence of big donors and increase the scope for candidates to compete on a small-scale but popular level. Limited to contributions from New York City residents and linked to agreed limited total candidate expenditures, it increases the onus on political entities informing and engaging with the public.

Electoral Finance and the Ministerial Mindset

Candidate selection in the developed world is generally focused around a long term commitment to a political party, either in ideals or professional employment, or a strong track record in another professional discipline. In developing countries, electoral candidates are more likely to emerge from local power bases involving elements of the informal sector or practices of corruption. This tends to exclude those with adequate education, training and professional expertise. As a consequence, the scenarios available for electoral finance in developing countries are less condusive to the selection of professionals suited to government that is transparent and forward-thinking, and more likely to stray into decision-making tainted by favouritism and concerns outside of the wider national interest.

It is therefore imperative that alternative means are pursued to encourage the best candidates for the job into government. As will be discussed later, this will require measures to encourage best practice amongst ministers, assessment of performance at an international level, and interaction between ministers of various nations to share their experiences and seek to build new professional standards.

The Politics of Water

In June 2003, Unique Production Company produced a series of programmes on the subject of the share of global water, which was broadcast globally by the BBC World Service. In that series, BBC news journalist Mike Embley investigated some of the biggest water life-cycle issues that affect the world today. The issues are truly global, as the series of programmes illustrates, covering the Middle East, Namibia in southern Africa, the vast resources of

Russia, and the US-Mexico border. The programme highlighted "the dividing issues and common themes surrounding this vital liquid" by hearing from those immediately and critically affected by its availability and use. One of the issues raised time and again is the political aspect of water—who gets access and who does not. It shows the real life-changing consequences of these decisions and provides a wide range of opinion—from politicians, businessmen, scientists and professionals on the ground. What emerges is a picture of a complex yet fundamentally critical and immediate issue for mankind.

The importance of professional judgement, long-term thinking, and actions based on the wider national interest are clearest witnessed through the examination of particular issues. It is here that one can fully extend the implications of ministerial deficiency and the necessity for improved ministerial effectiveness in the interests of the people of the world. Perhaps no subject requires more skill in judgement and long term planning than the politics of water. As Steinberg and Clark relate, "few resource conflicts better express the connection between social power and environmental transformation than controversies surrounding the construction and maintenance of water distribution networks."[18]

Water is the most essential and most awkward of natural resources. It has no substitute but many uses—for drinking, irrigation, transportation, satiation, energy production, agriculture, industrial process and every single activity of life. Water's usability depends not only on its quantity, but also on its quality, source, dependability and channels of supply.

Peter Mollinga has highlighted the essential political nature of water resource management.[19] The expansion of this field of study signifies the increased complexity and importance of the subject, and reflects the enormous intellectual capacities, judgement and time required for government ministers to manage this decision-making process effectively. The very aspect of conserving and distributing a nation's freshwater resources is one of the principle responsibilities of the state. Where in prior times where there was a relatively sufficient resource, though perhaps not in terms of supply management, this often appeared to be a naturally resolving function. However, given increased population numbers and per capita use, more intrusive and technical extraction methods reaching new sources, and the progressive drying up of sources due to overuse, climate change, melting snow caps and desertification, this resource requires more concerted, pro-active and engaged oversight. Serious concern must be taken to assess the measure of extraction and its nature and distribution along vast infrastructure projects from sources that include river systems, lakes, reservoirs, aquifers, rainfall and desalination plants.

The complicated nature is further enhanced by what Mollinga describes as "the 'problemsheds' or 'issue networks' of water resources management [which] may stretch well beyond the physical boundaries of these units, and span the globe and history."[20] Water is politically contested both within and outside of state governance, thereby requiring a nuanced engagement on political, as well as technical, levels. These correspond to four primary domains, as identified by Mollinga, constituting "the everyday politics of water, the politics of water policy in the context of sovereign states, inter-state hydropolitics, and the global politics of water."[21] This requires engagement not only on a technical level, but a political level that acknowledges responsibility for fair use that is not determined by affiliations, loyalty or corruption. It also requires a long-term conservation of the resource for future generations and for sustainability, which in itself is not a new determination but a historically founded and proven principle of society. The question is whether the ministerial mindset as currently exists has propelled the correct individuals into power, with the appropriate awareness and support structures, to perpetuate freshwater resources as a source of stable and continuing civilisation.

The politics of water is one of the great emerging themes of the 21st century, but its impact on geopolitics and conflict in the 20th century has already illustrated its capacity for generating international flashpoints. The conflict in Kashmir is one generally recognised as a conflict over territory and religion, which has spilled over to encompass disturbances and consequences across India, Pakistan and the wider region. However water, and access to it, functions as one of the key motivating factors in stirring tensions.

The headwaters of the Indus River, which runs 3,200 km through Pakistan, emerges from the region of Kashmir, through the Indus itself and its Jhelum, Chenab, Sutlej, Ravi and Beas tributaries. In all instances, these rivers run downstream from India into the territory of Pakistan, thus leaving India in an advantageous position when it comes to controlling their discharge. The Indus is the very lifeline of Pakistan, the only river running through the country that is classified as 92% arid or semi-arid. Yet the river basin extends beyond the borders of Pakistan, with 20% of the catchment area lying in India (predominantly the Punjab, known as the 'bread basket' of India, producing a fifth of the country's wheat), 5% in Afghanistan and 15% in Tibet.[22] In a land of want, it is the source of life and livelihoods. It is no wonder that control of the river is a matter of the very survival of the regions that survive on it. When during the early disputes of Kashmir, India closed off the Central Bari Doab Canal during the sowing season, thus setting Pakistan's harvest to ruin, it showed that it had the means to turn off the tap. Control of rivers left Pakistan's life in India's hands—and the Pakistani authorities have not forgotten this fact. No solution in Kashmir is possible unless Pakistan can be certain that the flow of water from the Indus river system is determined, always and at once, by mechanism that will not allow such a situation to repeat itself.

This calls, not only for national determination of river flow and management, but for wider agreement by all countries within the river basin. For while rivers only flow through countries and are not solely contained by them, states have traditionally been given major rights to manipulate the water passing through their territories. Both Pakistan and India have constructed dams to harness the power of water through electricity generation stations, as well as diverting the flow to support agricultural and industrial production. In times past, while the level of technological advancement did not allow for massive containment and diversion of flow, there may have been enough for all to share, but in the present era the pressures on water are multiplied. The Indus Water Treaty of 1960 gave exclusive control of the Indus, Jhelum and Chenab to Pakistan, and the Sutlej, Ravi and Beas to India. However the mounting pressures on water, due to rising populations and large-scale hydroelectric and irrigation programmes, have resulted in renewed tensions over the past two decades.

The Indus has been used as a tool for geopolitical ambitions rather than as a source for harmony and closer cooperation. Yet the relationship between the two countries is marred by distrust on both sides. India maintains it has never deliberately tampered with the supply, yet because of the surrounding mistrust it fails to share key river data.[23] Meanwhile in the middle lies Kashmir, a region with a growing frustration that it is unable to utilise its water resources for its own benefit. While it can be seen to be in one country's interest to absorb the majority of water flow for its own purposes, the creation of an unstable neighbour has serious political, social and security consequences, while the development of drought conditions can exacerbate the spread of arid conditions that characterise the shared downstream border. The question is, can the symbol and actualities of the river, which highlights the condition of the interconnectedness of society and ecology across territories, be harnessed in the same manner as states have sought to do with the water itself? Can a ministerial mindset be framed that recognises the former as much as the latter, with the effect that the benefits to both societies are readily accessed?

The evidence from history, from the distant past to the here and now, is that a different mindset can create conditions of plenty. Small water catchment projects adjusted to work with the seasons, and a recognition of the needs of those throughout the river system, can create flourishing conditions that support sustainable life: life that does not create conditions of insecurity, political tension, ecological destitution and social failure.

No country more exemplifies the contradictions of water in current usage—that of plenty and deprivation—than Bangladesh. The country is crisscrossed by 800 rivers that stretch for over 24,140 km and the southern region lies on a river delta spilling out into the Indian Ocean. Within this ecological system, Bangladesh suffers variously from cycles of flooding and drought, and a shortage of clean drinking water.

Many of its rivers are however now shrinking in depth and running dry. The Ganges runs from the foothills of the Himalayas through northern India before passing into Bangladesh. The Gangetic Basin, extending over 814,800 km^2, is home to 450 million people who rely on it for all aspects of life, yet this mighty river runs almost dry as it ends it enters the Bay of Bengal.[24] This has implications not only for water access, but for increased salinity in the ecologically valuable coastal delta region as freshwater flow declines.[25]

In 1961 construction began in India on the Farakka Barrage to divert 1,200 cubic metres per second of water from the Ganges to the Hooghly River for the purpose of reviving the Port of Kolkata, which had suffered from the accumulation of silt. The barrage, which was completed in 1975, runs 2,240 metres across the river and lies just 16.5 km from the Bangladeshi border. The effect of the construction by India was to divert river water directly from Bangladesh to West Bengal, yet it also harnesses this vital resource for agriculture, industry and the port's waterways, including the Farakka Super Thermal Power Station and through canals for farmers across the rice-cultivating region.

Yet the problems facing the Port of Kolkata are terminal and despite the huge expense and resources diverted to the construction of the barrage itself, port traffic is now shifting to Haldia in recognition of this. At the same time, rising levels of silt have begun to affect Bangladesh's waterways and ports. Discussions on both sides have been focused solely on water share, rather than trying to farm greater capacity in coordination with Nepal. Biswas, Nakayama and Uitto have observed that the water resources of the Ganges remain plentiful, but the concern lies during the dry season (see figure 4).[26] While discharge during the monsoon season has increased, ecological and agricultural resources have been negatively affected by low flows during the lean season. As little as 5% of the total annual flow would address several of the key ecological issues in this period, however this requires cooperation, coordination, the sharing of cross-border information which both countries have so far been reluctant to provide, and action to construct storage and catchment mechanisms. While temporary agreements between the two countries exist, including the obligation for India to provide 35,000 cusec of water for Bangladesh up until 2020, India absorbs over half of water share despite common international agreements limiting upper-riparian water extraction to 20-25%. This guideline has informed the water sharing treaties between India and Pakistan over the Indus, and between Egypt and Sudan over the Nile.

Figure 3: Annual minimum water level of the Ganges at
Hardinge Bridge (1965-1993)

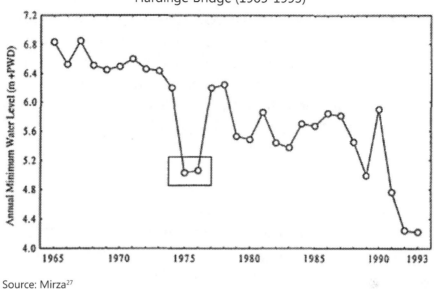

Source: Mirza[27]

Figure 4: Mean monthly minimum discharge of the Ganges at
Hardinge Bridge during the dry season (November-May)

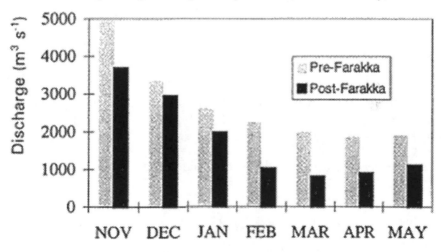

Source: Mirza[28]

With half the Indian population and a third of the Bangladeshi population living in the Ganges river basin, the importance of resolving this issue with foresight and longevity in mind is critical to their future national prosperity and well being. The example of the Gorai River, the major distributary serving the south-west region of Bangladesh, is instructive. Since the construction of the Farakka Barrage, monthly discharge levels have fallen between 57-72%,[29] with 40% of floodplains in the country having been affected. Meanwhile fish stocks in the Ganges have tumbled, with the recorded annual catch at Padma of the staple anadromous hilsa fish, whose progress up the river has been blocked by the barrage, declining from 4,193 metric tonnes in 1983-84 to 282 metric tonnes a decade later.[30] As Wolf writes, "Adverse effects in Bangladesh resulting from reduced upstream flow have included degradation of both surface and groundwater, impeded navigation, increased salinity, degraded fisheries, and danger to water supplies and public health."[31] Local populations have migrated out of the affected areas, with many taking refuge in India, highlighting that the consequences cannot be solely contained within national boundaries, but spill out across the region as a whole.

In 1996, a Water Sharing Agreement was reached between India and Bangladesh, but excluding Nepal, China and Bhutan.[32] As such the allocation of water was agreed as indicated in figure 5 below.

Figure 5: Agreed Water Sharing Allocations on the Ganges

Flow Amount	India	Bangladesh
Below 70,000 cusecs	50%	50%
70,000-75,000 cusecs	Balance of flow	35,000 cusecs
Above 75,000 cusecs	40,000 cusecs	Balance of flow

Source: Wolf and Newton[33]

However, the agreement was based on water discharge data from 1949 to 1988, since when levels have fallen markedly. Having made the political breakthrough of agreeing allocation shares, ministers failed to ensure that the information on which it was based was current and relevant. For the agreements on water allocations relate to shares of discharge at Farakka Barrage.[34] It failed to recognise that draws of water upstream have multiplied in recent decades, in India and Nepal, thus lowering the flow by the time it reaches Farakka Barrage. As such, India's allocation of water is regulated only once the remainder has approached the border of Bangladesh.

The importance of determining astute international and domestic policies is raised not only by management of the post-Farakka situation, but also by the repetition of events. In the face of protests from local indigenous people in its far eastern corner and from Bangladesh, India is proposing the construction of the Tipaimukh Dam in Manipur State, with a view to containing floodwaters and providing electricity generation. Despite Indian assurances of the benefits to be derived by Bangladesh, one of the members of the Joint River Commission has stated that Bangladesh did not receive its fair share of water from the Ganges in nine out of the 12 years preceding 2009.[35] India has so far failed to provide adequate access to information to its neighbour regarding key data, while the basic facts remain unchanged: siphoning off water will have consequences for its lower riparian neighbour, including hindering the spread of fertile sediment in the agricultural floodplains, as well as increasing salinity and silting up its coastal ports.

The issue therefore is not of one particular country, but recognition of the complexity and multiple layers of issues surrounding water and river management. The question is how is it possible to combine this comprehension with the relative ignorance on such issues of ministers, the political pressures, and personal idiosyncrasies? It becomes clear therefore that such decisions, which affect not only present populations, but ecological balances and the foundations for future economic prosperity and well-being, cannot be left to individuals without the correct mindset, appreciation and interest to deal with them. It cannot be left to the mindset that knows only best about winning elections, holding political sway, siphoning off money from economies and building power bases. Surmising the practice of one issue in a particular region of the globe demonstrates the absurdity and destructiveness of society led by those incapable and unwilling to face the seriousness of the issues confronting local, regional and global populations. To create the mindset, to create the minister, requires attracting the right candidates, enabling their passage to power, and providing the training and support to assist in these complex and important tasks.

The Northern Lights Politics

Dr. Charles Emmerson, the Australian born researcher, has completed extensive research on the Arctic region, its future prospects and the politics of sea resources. I had the happy opportunity to receive a signed copy of his book *The Future History of The Arctic* and to discuss with him these issues at an event organised by Chatham House in London. He has drawn a clear picture of geopolitics as it affects the Arctic Ocean, which matched many of my own concerns as I was writing my earlier book *Sustainable Development—A South Asian Perspective*, in which I emphasised the importance of doing business in a sustainable manner and in cognisance of the relationship to preserving water and air cleanliness.

What an image the Arctic presents. As we observe it on a globe it lies above us all. What portents and events flow from it, which are visited over all our heads. How symbolic this is, how the events that take place there, often beyond the realm of our notice, will affect us all. The melting of the polar ice cap will leech the water from millennia of glacial ice storage across the world's oceans, with concomitant effects for regional ecosystems and global weather patterns. But beyond our horizon, the unfreezing of the Arctic is opening up a new world to be explored, drilled and extracted, threatening one of the last clean and untapped regions that has for so long helped to regulate the global climate—from South America to Asia.

For the Arctic might appear remote, but at its door, which extends from North America to Europe to Asia, exist some of the most powerful and technologically advanced nations in the world. These are nations that do not always see eye-to-eye on ecological issues or political consensus. The challenge of reconciling the polities of the United States, Canada, Norway, Denmark and Russia is like an approaching iceberg, drifting ever closer, growing in magnitude, and presenting increasingly fewer options for manoeuvre. Perhaps more important, what lies below its waters is of global significance. The Arctic's neighbours seek control over the right to sell and profit from a region that in practice exists beyond their homeland, but to which international territorial law gives them rights of ownership. The tantalising riches below the ice have little chance of protection amidst the constant scrap for money.

The political feeding ground of the Arctic helped to prompt the drafting of the United Nations Convention on the Law of the Sea (UNCLOS) in 1982, which was eventually ratified in 1994. Its essential role is in determining sovereign claims pertaining to maritime concerns and, in particular, to the seabed. Given the extent of territory under examination and the distance from sovereign borders, the issue of the extension of sea shelves has become the primary focus of attention. Maritime law states that a nation has propriety over territorial waters that under normal circumstances extend 12 nautical miles from the coastlines. Beyond this an Exclusive Economic Zone exists wherein a state has the rights to exploit mineral and other resources extending up to 200 nautical miles from the coastline. However technological and conceptual innovation has introduced a new factor, that of the extended continental shelf, which redefines previous categorisation relating to sovereign rights.[36] This requires validated proof of a contiguous seabed extending from territorial waters, and enables economic rights to be widened as a consequence. Alongside the increasing frailty of the ice caps, with the development of new technology, such as increasingly more advanced submarines, GPS mapping equipment and more durable ice-breakers, the secrets of the Arctic Ocean are increasingly open to reach and their coordinates to be plotted. These require highly expensive underwater explorative operations, but are necessary when submitting applications for jurisdiction to UNCLOS for judgement. By providing evidence of extended continental shelves, countries are able to extend their zones of economic influence, with rights covering the seabed and the resources present below it.

This modern day feeding frenzy is indicative of the ecological dimensions that pertain to it. The slow build-up of material resources over millennia, in the forms of oil, gas and a multitude of other minerals, is suddenly seized upon, within a brief window of opportunity—both for categorisation: UNCLOS allows a 10-year period for asserting territorial claims upon ratification by each nation; and for consumption. What took millions of years to develop will be assessed, extracted, consumed and pumped out within a period of a few hundred. The shrinking of the Arctic Sea ice, by as much as 50% since the 1950's according to the U.S. National Snow and Ice Data Center,[37] far from being seen as a catastrophe that will impact on regions across the world, is welcomed as an economic opportunity by politicians, opening up a wealth of resources estimated to contained a quarter of current global oil and gas reserves.

The need, more acute than ever before, is to nurture a ministerial mindset that can meet these issues on the level required by humanity. Ministers now have evermore capacity to sanction the spoilage of perfectly functioning ecosystems and to drain resources that have taken tens of millions of years to accumulate, whether this be oil reserves under the Arctic seabed or aquifers below the Sahara Desert. A mindset based upon local and short-term economic benefit, the usage of resources carved up for a few that ought to exist for the entire world, and the failure to consider future generations for whom these resources will no longer exist—this presents the greatest threat to the quality of life for mankind. The greatest challenge is to affirm a mindset in which the priority is the careful management of resources, in both supply and demand.

On a less ambitious level, there exists scope for cooperation in the extraction of these resources among Arctic states. Given the present unlikelihood to extend the Antarctic Treaty, which limits exploration activity, to the north pole, whatever agreement is reached will be a modern day Berlin Conference of 1884-85, in which the continent of Africa was formally carved up amongst the European powers. This appears the most likely scenario, with states establishing joint exploration agreements that avoid legally delineating final maritime boundaries among the competitors.

The melting of the Arctic ice cap also presents increased opportunities for transportation. Given the varying rates of melt across the region, the Northern Sea Route, which passes along various routes above Siberia between Novaya Zamlya and the Bering Strait, currently presents the most viable option.[38] The difficult process of establishing the long-desired North-West

Passage across Canadian Waters and beyond Alaska is less advanced. However both require the continuation of ice cap melting before this trade can become established.

The Northern Sea Route, though carrying a small amount of intercontinental traffic at present, will require considerable capital investment in order to enable it to become a viable alternative to the Suez Canal. However, along with climactic conditions, geopolitical forces appear to moving in a favourable direction for Russia. The Suez Canal is currently beset by ongoing security concerns regarding instability in the Arab world and hostility to the West, the continued threat of Islamic terrorism, and the emergence of sophisticated piracy networks off the coast of Somalia that now extend deep into the Indian Ocean. While these issues may be resolved in time, the Suez route is constrained by capacity issues that limit the number and size of ships through the canal. As ships grow increasingly in size and global trade rises, the bottleneck will begin to present serious concerns.

These difficulties are helping to turn the tide of opinion towards the gamble of identifying secure routes, building ice-capable shipping, and developing new port facilities for the Northern Sea Route. Traffic along the route peaked in 1987, however the collapse of the Soviet-Russia economy precipitated a decline in cargo movements and capital maintenance that has yet to be fully reversed. The prospect also poses a tantalising geopolitical question. The route was officially opened to international traffic in 1991. Will a flourishing Northern Sea Route bring Russia into closer cooperation with the West by exposing its hidden coastline, or enable it to create further distance on the basis of secured revenue streams, as is presently the case with its gas and oil revenues? Lawson Brigham writes that this closed and security-sensitive region is developing into "a vast marine area more open for use, and, potentially, integrated with the world economy".[39] If so, the transformation of the Arctic from a Cold War militarised backwater into an open internationally-accessed zone will enable friendlier relations that may encourage agreed resource use as well.

Yet as ever, more optimistic assessments run aground against *realpolitik*. Russia is seeking to maintain control over management of the proposed route while it has yet to divert funds to the enormous project. More worryingly, the waters themselves are contested, with the United States and the European Union claiming the route passes through international waters, while China also is pressing claims to both the Northern Sea Route and North-West Passage. Margaret Blunden writes, "One possible scenario of Chinese naval vessels, tasked with protecting Chinese merchant ships, in the seas north of Russia or in the North Atlantic, would confront Russia and NATO with a challenging new security environment."[40]

Maritime trade amongst the 27 countries of the European Union amounted to 3.8 billion tonnes in 2006 and is estimated to grow to 5.3 billion tonnes by 2018.[41] The importance of the sea trade is growing, not declining, as the global economy expands and diversifies. Arctic sea routes also reflect an increasing change in the focus of trade, moving northwards as China replaces its more southern Asian neighbours as the engine of growth. This is important for transportation considerations, as it changes the balance of relative distance between destinations, slowly but ever more favourably shortening northerly sea routes. In this, the trade between two of the powerhouses of the global economy is indicative and influential. Between 2000 and 2009, the Chinese share of imports into Germany rose from a third to a half, while the share of German exports heading to China rose from 9% in 2002 to 22% by 2009.[42] In 2001, the Chinese prime minister Wen Jiabao predicted trade between China and Germany could double within five years,[43] while the shorter trade route through the Arctic could bring Germany profits of up to half a million euros per delivery by large container ship.[44] It is therefore not surprising that the European Union has been seeking to intervene in the issue, to secure the Arctic region as an international zone, in the German view as "the common heritage of mankind",[45] though this has not prevented a stepping up in joint military exercises between Germany and Scandinavian nations. However, the countries bordering the Arctic are resistant to such intervention, arguing that if the region is opened to all countries, the same standards should be enacted elsewhere.

The prospect of the remote region, although one predicted to bring future riches, being a source for conflict must focus minds. The issues of the future, though uncertain, are nonetheless clearly delineated. It contrasts to the circumstances of the Ganges basin, a high-density region whose resources have been shared, carved up and debated for decades. What brings commonality to both regions and to both tasks—characterised by very different conditions—is to devise a way to achieve agreed, mutually supportive and sustainable solutions. To accommodate the challenges presented at both ends of this scale requires discipline of the mind and endeavour, rather than short-term accommodations. It requires a ministerial mindset that is firm upon the principles required of it, and enveloped by suitable knowledge and a willingness to engage with a wide range of expert opinion.

PART 2

Ministers as Funambulists

By Mark T Jones

The fact that in the majority of legislative structures most if not all appointments are of a political nature means that those in office are constrained by party political obligations and expectations. Those individuals awarded appointments are invariably selected on the expectation that either they will merely sit and occupy the position for the length of their tenure or implement directives that generally are not of their own making. Such is the jaundiced view that society has of politicians that few individuals recognize the potential for politics and therefore politicians to be agents of positive change. Caroselli reminds us that politics can be a means of affecting positive change; "Politics can be seen as a way to make the impossible possible, the imagined real, and the scorned proud again." (Caroselli 2003: 61)[46] The thrust of her argument lies with the pivotal role of effective communication. Politicians, and for good or ill, all Ministers are deemed politicians first and ministers second, are required to give thought to how their words will be interpreted or, more often than not, misinterpreted. Caroselli stresses the importance of the effect of spoken and written communication, something Ministers the world over often give insufficient thought to. "The egocentric leader believes the world revolves around his or her own concerns." (Caroselli 2003: 63)[47] and the same is often deemed to be true of Ministers.

Existing ministerial structures are rarely designed to liberate, their constraining nature ensures that those appointed stay within a given brief and thus invariably maintain the *status quo*. Governments generally prefer a safe pair of hands to over-active individuals, who might in some way upset the equilibrium. Charisma is often deemed a dangerous thing, not least because it potentially threatens to overshadow those who occupy the highest public office in the land. If governments are fearful of colourful characters on a mission to get things done the danger is that they end up with bland individuals who give the impression of being largely inert and, as such, ineffective. Such apparent inactivity can be equally dangerous as it leaves Administrations open to the charge of inactivity based on inability, nepotism or some other bias centred upon ethnicity, clan/tribal loyalty or religious or regional affiliation. Essentially the challenge facing all governmental structures is comparable to that of the tightrope walker.

So what precisely are the qualities required of these latter-day Blondins that we expect so much of? A successful funambulist (tightrope walker) requires a number of characteristics, none of which on their own will guarantee their success or longevity. If for a moment we think of Ahdili Wuxiuer (better known as Adil Hoshur), a current Guinness World Record Holder who is a practitioner of *dawaz*—the Uyghur tradition of high wire walking, we can concentrate our mind on what would be required to execute such a hair raising feet with aplomb. Whilst there could be some debate around the precise qualities and attributes required, the following are certainly essential:

> ambition, application, conviction, courage, judgement, mental and physical agility as well nerves of steel

Those seeking or being called to high office are similarly exposing themselves to danger and equally they require an in-depth understanding of the risks and challenges they face and an appreciation of that which is possible and that that which is extremely unlikely. The analogy of the tightrope walker is a pertinent one, not least because a range of other factors come into play (See Fig. 1 Jones' Octagon of Success).

Figure 6: Jones' Octagon of Success (JOOS)

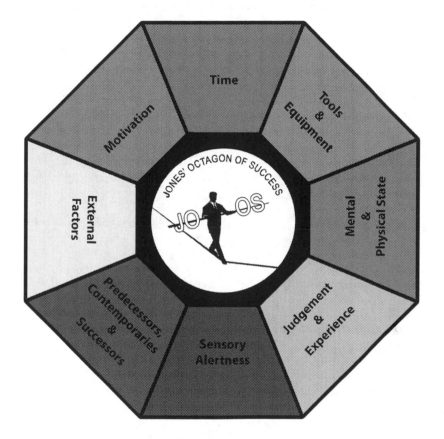

Time

The constraints of time are a constant complaint of all ministries and of governments in particular when criticised by various stakeholders. That said, there is something extremely democratic about the modern concept of time in its daily sense, and that is that we all have the same allocation regardless of our position in the scheme of things. Time optimisation is an issue that warrants the attention of all in government. Attitudes to time vary enormously, with some cultures and nationalities deemed to have a more rigid sense of time and especially punctuality. Some such as the British are said to live in a society seemingly dominated by horological slavery, whilst elsewhere the approach to time is much more relaxed. Anolue argues that attitudes to what she dubs Africa Time need to change, she goes on to acknowledge cultural differences, but makes a cogent argument that change lies through a generational shift; "To sort out our abuse of time is the task that must be done. It is left to our young future leaders to take the bull by the horns; they are the ones that can make the difference where we have failed." (Anolue 2012: 17)[48]

Most governments live by their own particular clock and that is the election cycle and thus this particular time frame dominates thinking. Normally, Administrations serve four, five or six years and their prime objective is to see out their full term and if possible be re-elected. Ministerial appointments do not always last for the whole of that timeframe and as a result there are various limitations on what can be achieved or indeed should be expected of a minister and their staff. Governmental priorities soon make it clear that even individual ministerial objectives can become marginalized, and in some ways relegated. A look at the Government of Somaliland's Government Priorities for the 2013-2014 Development Sector[49] are just as telling about what does not feature as to what is included. The seven ministerial committees established by President Ahmed Mahmoud Silanyo in October 2012 are as follows:

1) 2013 National Annual Budget (11)*
2) Judiciary Reform Committee (6)
3) Eastern Regions Conflict Resolution Committee (10)
4) Public Property Management Reform Committee (8)
5) Foreign Affairs Policy Committee (10)
6) National Food Security Committee (10)
7) Job Creation Committee (10)
    *The number in brackets indicates the number of individuals that make up each committee.

With a number of ministers and deputy ministers sitting on more than one committee it becomes immediately apparent that time is going to be a key factor, as is the need to ensure that the relevant ministers are properly briefed so as to contribute in a constructive manner. Hargeisa, Somaliland's capital city, is fortunate in having relatively few traffic problems, which means in theory at least ministerial meetings can start on time. With a Government consisting of three branches: the Executive Branch (The President, the Vice President and the Cabinet), the Legislative Branch (The House of Representatives and the House of Elders) and the Judicial Branch, the calls on the time of ministers are extensive, with protocol demanding that office holders are frequently expected to accompany the President on his peregrinations throughout the country and further afield, as well as being available to meet, greet and entertain visiting dignitaries.

From the moment a minister is appointed, he or she is expected to hit the ground running and rapidly assimilate their brief. Precious little time is given over to the acclimatisation process, for many new ministers it is a question of sink or swim, with some having never been taught to swim in the first place. Imagine the degree of trepidation that 64 year old Mohamed Ibrahim must have felt when in the autumn of 2011 he went from being a learning support assistant in a North London School to being Deputy Prime Minister of the Transitional Federal Government in Somalia. In his resignation letter to the Headmaster of the School where he was working he wrote: "I was unexpectedly called to my country Somalia during the school holidays and appointed as a deputy prime minister and the minister for foreign affairs at a time when the country was facing humanitarian crises such as drought and famine."[50] Here was a classic case of in at the deep end. Whilst such a change is relatively extreme, it is not as unusual as some might believe and highlights the steep learning curve faced by those called upon to serve their country.

In the United Kingdom the response received to a request from a member of public under the Freedom of Information Act (2000) about government policy regarding MPs and ministerial training indicates that even in highly complex and highly developed parliamentary systems there is more than an element of time being of the essence:

The Government recognises that training for Ministers can help develop their skills. An induction workshop for Ministers new to government is held after general elections and major reshuffles, departments run structured, individual induction programmes for Ministers new in post and the National School of Government (NSG) works with the Cabinet Office to provide the Ministerial programme which is tailored to the needs of individual ministers.[51]

Time-keeping and time management are issues that some ministers with an inflated view of their own importance take little cognisance of. There are some individuals who mistakenly believe that an indication of their new found power is the ability to keep people waiting. Effective ministers recognize that an important corollary of ministerial power is ministerial responsibility. With new found status comes the danger of becoming detached from those one is chosen to serve. Advisors and sycophants compete for attention and pay scant regard to those who they deem too lowly to matter. Making time for cleaners, drivers, guards and clerks can help ensure a handle on what is really going on outside the political bubble of high office. The staff that make the tea, sweep the courtyard or act as couriers are citizens, maybe voters, and often have a far better appreciation of inflationary pressures as well as the *vox populi.* By investing time and courtesy in all staff a minister earns respect rather than merely expecting it because they have the title Honourable Minister for an allotted time.

Those that carry the ministerial mantle would do well to set aside some time each day for the following:

- Gauging the morale and mood of the ministerial support team
- Monitoring good practice from comparable ministries internationally
- Perusing scope for ensuring that the ministerial writ is acted upon beyond the confines of the capital and its environs
- Ensuring that grievances and complaints are examined with objectivity and all possible speed
- Examining the ways in which the ministry is communicating its aspiration and endeavours to stakeholders

Ministers are in a position to effect positive change and should they choose to exercise this power and responsibility they may help provide both the moral scaffolding and the impetus to enable governments to improve the lives of citizens. Inactivity, indifference, and ignorance can all conspire to ensure that in an allotted period of time precious little is achieved. The Institute for Security Studies in *Sierra Leone—A country review of crime and criminal justice, 2008* (123)[52] explains the lack of progress thus: "The challenges posed by institutional inertia of such government departments as Sierra Leone's Ministries of Foreign Affairs and of Justice partly explain the failure of the country to ratify some of the conventions and protocols. Clearly an inadequate amount of time has been allocated to such matters, the review notes that incredibly Sierra Leone has still yet to get around to ratifying the Slavery Convention (121-122)[53] The ability to acknowledge and act on an issue is one that can not only earn respect and plaudits, but also helps ensure that an issue gains a wider understanding. 2004 saw the first meeting of the Coordinated Mekong Ministerial Initiative against Trafficking (COMMIT) held in Rangoon (Yangon), Burma (Myanmar)[54] and is an example of how ministers can use their time to help tackle complex transnational problems. People trafficking is one that warrants a thorough appraisal of the facts and this can only be done providing there is adequate briefing, preparation and, above all, else will.

Constituents, committees and innumerable functions all place considerable demands on a minister's time. Elected officials cannot afford to ignore or neglect those that elected him or her, as there may come a time when the patronage they enjoy in office suddenly comes to an end. Patronage is not too strong a word and this too reminds ministers and budding ministers that they must not forget those who have brought them into the Cabinet. Committees, whilst tiresome allow Ministers to influence policy and occasionally even help shape priorities. Pressing issues such as water security can be championed with a vengeance.

China, India, the UK and the USA are among a number of leading countries who currently do not have a single city or region as a signatory of the Istanbul Water Consensus (IWC). Brisbane is the only city from Australia to have signed, whilst in contrast Brazil and

France have embraced the IWC with a real passion as well as cities and regions from 22 African countries having signed.[55]

To the overworked Minister, and indeed some are over worked whilst others are under employed, there are countless functions and visits to perform. These activities afford an opportunity to take the political pulse, as well as to be seen and articulate the Government's vision, achievements and occasionally short-comings. Ministerial cars and the purple prose of welcome speeches are a danger in that they deflect the Minister from the job in hand. Chauffeurs and fine words are all very well, but they do not advance policy. Rather than a minister counting how many seats they are placed away from the President at an official function, it would be better to reflect on how to ensure a timely delivery of projects, that are on or even under budget—now that would be time well spent.

Experience and Judgement

Different traditions of government mean that in some states there exist elites that expect to hold high office. Naturally within such structures the prevailing culture is one that inculcates core codes and values from an early age and endeavours to reinforce these through social norms and expectations. Hereditary or quasi-hereditary governmental structures raise interesting questions about societal expectations and whether systems are willing or able to adapt, or are innately monolithic. Those individuals destined to high office often find that whilst they may be fast tracked because of who they are or who they are related to, the same also needs to exist in regard to ministerial delivery. A case in point is that of H.E. Sheikh Abdullah bin Zayed Al-Nahyan (30/04/1972), the current Foreign Minister of the United Arab Emirates (UAE). As the son of the founder of the UAE and its first

President from an early age he was marked out for a life of service. He read Political Science at the United Arab Emirates University and graduated in 1995 and was immediately appointed Under Secretary of the Ministry of Information and Culture. Less than two years later he was promoted to Minister of Information and Culture and amongst his other responsibilities held and continues to hold the Chairmanship of the Board of the National Media Council. By all accounts he has given a creditable account of himself and early in 2006 he was appointed Minister of Foreign Affairs. Whilst family connections have ensured a smooth and in some ways meteoric rise to high office, the pressures and expectations still exist. As a Minister he is still expected to have a firm handle on his brief, understand internal and external dynamics and endeavour to master the complexities of a rapidly changing geo-political landscape in an era that has witnessed the Arab Spring, civil war in Syria and on-going tension between Shi'a and Sunni Muslims. Each day presents fresh challenges and for such a Minister the learning has been of the baptism of fire variety. Yes, there will have been older heads to turn to for wise counsel, but had he not been able to assimilate what was required at speed he would soon have found himself moved sideways rather than promoted. One of the flaws that are more likely to exist in dynastic governmental systems is nepotism—that said, such a weakness is not unique to such a system. All ministries have the potential to be places of intrigue where disorder often reigns supreme, yet with coolness and circumspection there is no reason to suppose that the camarillas that seek to influence ministers cannot be held in check.

When Francois Hollande was elected President of France in 2012 he assumed the role as Head of State having had no ministerial experience. When he assembled his cabinet he chose to appoint a number of experienced individuals, whilst appointing Jean-Marc Ayrault, a little-known figure with no ministerial experience as his Prime Minister. The issue of experience is a thorny one that frequently raises hackles. *The Copenhagen Post (21/09/2012)* elucidated something of the experience gap which is believed to exist in the current Danish Government with particular reference to its understanding of the world of work and the shaping of a strategy to generate greater employment:

In total, seven of the country's 23 ministers have not had a real-world job since completing their education, while another four ministers have under five years of experience in the job market. While the job market is the government's stated top priority, only 12 ministers have over five years of experience on their CV.[56]

As well as the paper going on to highlight how few ministers and MPs had experience of the world of work it also drew upon a recent report that concludes that many ministers are often detached from those they are elected to serve:

A study by think-tank Cevea from last year showed that 64 percent of MPs were academics. In the general public, academics only account for seven percent. Professor Niels Kærgård from the University of Copenhagen compared MPs' professional experience in 1966 to that of 2007. He believes that parliament has become an isolated bubble that has floated further and further away from voters.[57]

Lack of experience is an issue that has been used as a stick with which to beat ruling parties for many a year. When in 1852 Benjamin Disraeli served as Chancellor of the Exchequer of Great Britain, William Gladstone, the Leader of the Opposition made a point of drawing attention to Disraeli's lack of ministerial experience. 160 years later the President Michael Sata of Zambia made direct reference to the shortage of suitably qualified personnel on the day he appointed his first Cabinet; "Zambia at the moment has a problem. The problem we have in Zambia is we have people without any experience, people without any background come from nowhere . . ."[58] He went on to draw attention to the dearth of suitable talent in key ministries; "We have so many potholes in the Ministry of Home Affairs . . ." This familiar refrain raises legitimate questions about why bright people often shy away from high office. For some individuals the constant media scrutiny and brickbats mean that the cost both for them and their family is possibly too high. Some politicians prefer to keep a lower profile by serving on the backbenches, whilst those appointed to ministerial office are in greater need than ever of whatever scaffolding is available to support them in their duties. Other exceptional individuals believe that the prospects for preferment and generous remuneration packages are far more likely to be found in the private sector.

The ability to draw upon and utilise transferable skills is clearly important. Ministerial training can in part at least help harness and enhance the existing skill set that may enable the post holder to function more effectively. Knowing when to speak and when to remain silent is a life skill. Listening is a pre-requisite as is the ability to look as well as see. Ministers are invariably part of a collegiate decision-making process and this demands patience, the ability to fight one's corner (particularly with regard to ministerial staff and funding) as well as being prepared to compromise. Junior ministers have to be quick learners, and be prepared to accept that many governments function on the understanding that they operate along the lines of collective responsibility. It usually takes a while to realise that dissent does not necessarily mean or imply disloyalty, and this is equally true of ministerial staff as it is of ministers themselves. In Westminster style democracies responsibility takes two forms, that of collective and individual responsibility. Effective government requires those that exercise power to pay equal attention to the exercise of responsibility, something that takes discernment and fine judgement.

Ministers are expected to grow in experience and exercise judgement that demonstrates understanding and sagacity. Very rarely do ministers live up to society's expectations. Any form of induction or on the job training must also attune itself to shifting societal standards. Philip Johnson in an article entitled: *The end of ministerial responsibility* [59] contrasts changing attitudes by examining ministerial attitudes to personal responsibility. Johnson chooses to quote directly from Sir Thomas Dugdale's resignation address to the House of Commons when he resigned as Minister of Agriculture in 1954; "I, as minister, must accept full responsibility for any mistakes and inefficiency of officials in my department, just as, when my officials bring off any success on my behalf, I take full credit for them." He uses this quotation to hammer home his belief that ministerial standards in Britain have declined. He concludes with a damning critique of those in Government positions: "Vast sums of money have been wasted and people's lives blighted because of actions taken by or on behalf of ministers, who not only escape responsibility but are often promoted."

Even the most experienced and seemingly sure footed of ministers are indiscrete, make gaffs in front of the press or at the end of the long day at the office verbally lash out at a member of the public or in as in case of a senior British Politician at a Police Officer on duty at the gates of No 10 Downing Street.

All ministers whether new to the post or of considerable experience are pray to lobbying and the machinations of vested interests. It is difficult to escape those carefully choreographed visits to schools, factories and farms designed to show the Minister what it is thought they want to see. It is not necessarily a matter of ministers working harder, but working smarter. Objectivity, pragmatism and the ability to ask searching questions are essential requirements of ministers who aspire to be office holders that bring about a positive change. Positive change relies to a large degree on the issue of trust, often a rare commodity in political circles, but a prerequisite of real transparency. Transparency requires that ministerial dealings are open and objective, something that is easier said than done. In reality there are times when robust legislation finds itself diluted into mere recommendation, and regulatory bodies are emasculated or rendered ineffective. When the Ministry of the Environment and Forests, Bangladesh endeavoured to address the environmental degradation brought about by it being one of three countries that according to the World Bank[60] account for 70-80% of the global ship breaking and recycling industry (SBRI) representatives from the ship breakers successfully lobbied their way onto the committee designed to tackle the problem. With ship breaking a major industry in the environs of the Port City of Chittagong, as well as a key employer, it did not take the representatives of the industry long to scupper most of the safeguards that were being proposed for the sector. The ministerial high wire act is one that requires remarkable perspicacity and courage.

Motivation

Tightrope walkers have a point to prove to themselves and to others. Whilst undoubtedly some practise and preparation takes place out of the public eye, for their achievements to be truly recognised they need to be seen. The adrenalin rush and much of the thrill that undoubtedly acts as a driver when attempting such a difficult feat lies with achieving something against the odds. Those who put themselves up for public office have to be equally single minded and experience moments of intense elation when certain goals are achieved, whether they are being selected as a candidate, being elected or being called to serve in government.

For some the path to ministerial responsibility is undoubtedly easier than others. Up until April 2012 when his father Abdoulaye Wade failed to be re-elected as President of Senegal, Karim Wade (born 1968) was Minister of State, Minister of International Co-operation, Air Transport, Infrastructure and Energy. No matter how capable an individual, such an extensive portfolio raises questions about whether others could have brought their own strengths and insights to the task. Whilst most individuals who seek public office at a governmental level will undoubtedly subscribe to the notion of public service, the actuality is often more complex. No nation describes itself as a meritocracy and so the reasoning why certain individuals are appointed varies on a case-by-case basis. It has to be assumed that during their allotted tenure in office a minister will desire to bring about a positive change and therefore leave a positive legacy. Accepting an appointment is only the beginning; the Minister will have to motivate themselves and their staff, often against the odds. Some ministers have an over-inflated view of what they can achieve, only to be disillusioned once they discover the actuality of their remit. To a new or junior minister it can be a rude awakening to discover that decisions are frequently decided in Cabinet to which a minister finds themselves committed and yet may fundamentally disagree with or has at times had no direct say in. When it comes to issues related to the arms industry, national security and foreign policy matters often become even more opaque.

Training requires guidance and guidelines, which help provide an operational framework to enable ministers to channel their enthusiasm. The looser the framework, the greater the possibility that ministers and ministries will stray into areas that could be viewed as ethically suspect. Ministerial Codes are not there to be paid lip service to, but are a constant reminder of the responsibilities of high office. When we examine such a code we soon become aware of just how challenging living by such a code is.

The Seven Principles of Public Life, sometimes known as the Nolan principles:

- Selflessness—Holders of public office should act solely in terms of the public interest. They should not do so in order to gain financial or other benefits for themselves, their family or their friends.
- Integrity—Holders of public office should not place themselves under any financial or other obligation to outside individuals or organisations that might seek to influence them in the performance of their official duties.
- Objectivity—In carrying out public business, including making public appointments, awarding contracts, or recommending individuals for rewards and benefits, holders of public office should make choices on merit.
- Accountability—Holders of public office are accountable for their decisions and actions to the public and must submit themselves to whatever scrutiny is appropriate to their office.
- Openness—Holders of public office should be as open as possible about all the decisions and actions they take. They should give reasons for their decisions and restrict information only when the wider public interest clearly demands.
- Honesty—Holders of public office have a duty to declare any private interests relating to their public duties and to take steps to resolve any conflicts arising in a way that protects the public interest.
- Leadership—Holders of public office should promote and support these principles by leadership and example.[61]

Minister motivation takes on various forms; for some are scions of ministerial dynasties, the trappings of power and influence is a magnetic pull, whilst others are in the Disraelian mould and seek to ascend the greasy pole. Others end up in ministerial posts more by accident than design. Personal ambition and conflicting pressures are an integral part of the lot of those elected as Members of Parliament or Senators, something articulated by Hon. Benjamin Chikusa, the Member of Parliament for Dowa North in the Malawian Parliament:

MPs come under pressure from the executive to pass bills. Newly elected MPs are often easily influenced. Others are enticed by the prospect of cabinet posts and vote along party lines in order to position themselves favourably. As parliamentarians we are constantly trying to maintain a balance between addressing the expectations of our constituencies and fulfilling roles in parliament. If we are particularly outspoken we risk alienating ourselves. Restriction of district budget allocation has been used to control MPs. If this happens, it is ultimately our constituencies which suffer. (Chikaya-Banda, 2012:12)[62]

Ministers are not meant merely to maintain the *status quo*. In reality the Executive of some countries acts as a bulwark against change and seeks to appoint ministers who are pliant, biddable and some instances supine. Whatever their motivation, few ministers ever achieve all they set out to achieve, and from the outset have to be ready to make compromises and sacrifices which over time may dilute and occasionally sour the powerful elixir that took some of them into politics in the first place.

Tools and Equipment

Funambulists set out to complete their goal with a minimum of equipment. The art of maintaining balance whilst walking along a tensioned wire between two points can be done either using a tool for balance (a pole, fan, umbrella etc.) or freehand, using only one's body to maintain balance. The tools and equipment a government minister has at their disposal to endeavour to achieve all that they set out to achieve varies enormously. Certain ministries e.g. Defense receive sizeable budgetary allocations (Saudi Arabia 10.1; Oman 8.5 and Israel 6.5 as % of GDP in 2010)[63] The wide disparities between ministries, perceived ministerial status and fixed asset, budgetary and staffing allocations all impact on a ministry's ability to function effectively and efficiently. Whilst resources are important, cohesion, purpose and resource optimisation are all factors that have a bearing on a ministry's actual or perceived success. Just as a minister with eight mobile phones is no more likely to be any more efficient or effective than one with only one phone, the same, is true when it comes to ministries themselves. Some are often overly complex, even bloated in nature, with near impenetrable Kafkaesque bureaucracies thwarting the best endeavours of the most industrious and visionary of ministers. The challenges faced are many and varied, and at this juncture it would be useful to explore several examples of the types of problem that certain governments and their attendant ministries are expected to wrestle with.

Victoire Ndikumana—Ministry of Trade, Industry, Posts and Tourism in Burundi is candid in her assessment of the task facing her country:

Ministries in Burundi face a range of challenges. Capacity building is a major area that needs to be addressed. Currently there is a lack of suitably qualified staff to fill vacancies and this matter is made more problematic by the fact that relatively low salaries result in experienced and able personnel seeking to take up better remunerated posts elsewhere.

The Minister also acknowledges that whilst ministries are capable of initiating ideas and projects designed to improve the lot of citizens, many such projects are never acted upon due to lack of funds. With ministers having to manage extensive portfolios, the Government has endeavoured to help focus minds by organising government retreats on specific subjects, but it is aware that further specialist training is required if it to deliver on its Burundi Vision 2025 that includes a series of priorities including:

- Reconstructing national unity, peace and security
- Control demographic growth and improving food security
- Tackling the problem of unemployment, as well as boosting per capita incomes
- Diversifying the economy and improving competitiveness
- Developing the country's urban and rural infrastructure
- Improving national literacy and numeracy levels

Elsewhere in Africa the prolonged drought that has recently devastated Somalia, Somaliland and much of the Horn of Africa is likely to have a long-term impact. Pastoral and semi-pastoral communities have seen their lives blighted, with their livestock decimated as many traditional watering holes have long since dried up. The few *haro* (hand-dug wells) and *ella* (deep wells) along with various *berkads* (water cisterns) are largely empty or seriously depleted. Matters have been made worse by the loss of groundcover, especially trees which have been cut down for the production of charcoal for cooking (doubly sad as Somaliland has extensive bituminous and lignite coal deposits and is one of the optimum places on Planet Earth where photovoltaic cells could be employed). The destruction of trees and shrubs along with the over grazing of vegetation has resulted in the erosion of top-soil and thus the further impoverishment of the landscape. In countries such as Somaliland the effect has been devastating as pastoralists have been forced to drift into urban areas. The need for precious foreign currency sees the landscape of the Horn of Africa is being denuded of trees, especially *galool* (acacia bussei) in order to provide charcoal so that people in Saudi Arabia, the UAE and other Arab States can indulge their passion for smoking *shisha* (See Fig. 2 Charcoal from the Horn of Africa in the UAE).

To the outsider much of Somaliland's arid and semi-arid landscape appears as hostile to any form of farming as is a lunar landscape; this could not be further from the truth. Somalis have a wealth of knowledge and regional expertise that means that under normal circumstances they are well placed to maximise the land's potential. A case in point is that of apiculture (bee keeping), something which has long been integral to the lives of rural communities. Somalis appreciate the fact that the honey bee and the fruits of its labours has been appreciated for time in memorial, it even has its own *Sura* (Sura an-Nahl) in the *Qu'ran* 16:68:

> And your Lord taught the honey bee to build its cells in hills, on trees, and in (men's) habitations, and find with skills the spacious paths of its Lord there issues from within their bodies a drink of varying colours, wherein is healing for men: verily in this is a sign for those who give thought

Honey is famed the world over for its medicinal properties and apiculture yields other valuable products such as royal jelly (a natural anti-inflammatory that also acts as a bactericide as well as helping to lower cholesterol) and beeswax (ideal for making candles, body creams and shoe polish). Such a valuable crop deserves more widespread support and recognition. The quality of this product is such that with proper packaging and marketing it could easily find itself on the shelves of premium food emporiums internationally, thus generating valuable foreign currency for the economy.

In common with other aspects of agriculture, the drought and general land degradation has hit honey productivity. Many of the flowers, shrubs and trees that prove most attractive to bees are being lost to drought and to the perpetual quest for charcoal and grazing. Somaliland is remarkably biodiverse, but its rich flora and fauna is now under constant threat. If apiculture is to be maintained, consolidated and further developed there has to be a strategy that sees the establishment of 'vegetation corridors' and 'vegetation oases'; these not only become a haven for bees, but help support a range other insects, birds and other wildlife. Imagine if you will the landscape of the Horn devoid of the following:

Biological name	Common name in Somali
Conyza stricta	Hamur
Acacia seyal	Fulay
Grewia decidua	Ohop
Acacai nolotica	Tugar
Acacia mellifera	Bil'il

Institutions such as the University of Barao have already made a start in protecting Somaliland's plant diversity by establishing a seed bank. The Government of Somaliland could now champion beekeeping as a way of sustaining rural communities; it would do well to ensure that it encourages sustainable urban agriculture too. When it comes to Urban Agriculture, the undisputed capital in this regard is Cuba, where the inhabitants of Havana have learnt to capitalise on a rich farming heritage that has yielded remarkable economic, physical and psychological benefits. There is no reason to believe that Somalis cannot be just as ingenious as their Cuban counterparts, but to date neither ministries nor municipalities have taken the lead and provided suitable encouragement. Such topics as Urban Agriculture, along with permaculture are essential areas for research and instruction for specialists in food and farming at the country's universities and will require sustained investment in research and development. Leadership from central government and key ministries is crucial to food and bio security.

More effective water harvesting and management is going to be integral to progress in the field of all aspects of agriculture including beekeeping. Whilst efforts are being made to conserve and optimise water resources, these still appear to lack an effective co-ordinated approach. The gravity of the current situation begs the question as to whether the existing Ministry portfolios require some form of reappraisal and reorganisation. The Ministry of Agriculture and the Ministry of Livestock could easily be combined, whilst there is a convincing case for the establishment of a Ministry of Water and the Environment (something which exists in the UEA) with the existing Ministry of Water and Mineral Resources becoming the Ministry of Mines and Energy.

Somaliland like all mature nations will be required to learn lessons from elsewhere, but ultimately it will survive and prosper if it learns to fully harness the resourcefulness of its people in times of trial and tribulation. Just as the honeybee is industrious and has a sense of the communal good with clear and strong ministerial and communal leadership, Somalis would be better placed to rise to the challenge that faces them and adapt accordingly.

Whilst ministers will always bemoan their ministry's lack of equipment and resources, it is more a question of them understanding how to use resources in a judicious manner. New and existing ministers need to work assiduously to ensure that systems are in pace to minimise waste and to monitor procurement processes. Those charged with the responsibility of executing ministerial objectives have to be supported and imbued with the ministerial vision, if not they will drag their feet, and in so doing will undermine objectives and ultimately damage the minister's

combined tacit knowledge that enable its communication. For example, concepts, images, and written documents can support this kind of interaction. When tacit knowledge is made explicit, knowledge is crystallized, thus allowing it to be shared by others, and it becomes the basis of new knowledge. Concept creation in new product development is an example of this conversion process.

3. Explicit to Explicit (Combination)—Explicit to explicit by Combination (organizing, integrating knowledge), combining different types of explicit knowledge, for example building prototypes. The creative use of computerized communication networks and large-scale databases can support this mode of knowledge conversion. Explicit knowledge is collected from inside or outside the organisation and then combined, edited or processed to form new knowledge. The new explicit knowledge is then disseminated among the members of the organization.

4. Explicit to Tacit (Internalization)—Explicit to tacit by Internalization (knowledge receiving and application by an individual), enclosed by learning by doing; on the other hand, explicit knowledge becomes part of an individual's knowledge and will be assets for an organization. Internalization is also a process of continuous individual and collective reflection and the ability to see connections and recognize patterns and the capacity to make sense between fields, ideas, and concepts.[64]

Figure 7: The SECI Model

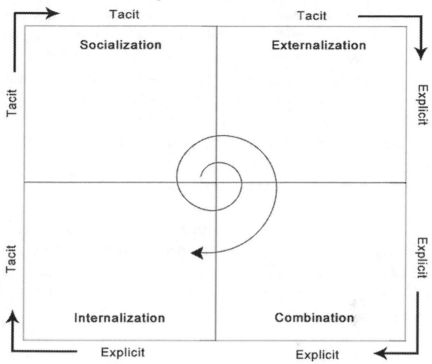

Governments have their own mental and physical state and this
is a fact that no budding minister can afford to ignore. Some
Administrations begin with a substantial mandate from the
electorate and depending on what proceeds it is afforded a deep
well of goodwill. The honeymoon period and the air of expectation
affords a government and individual ministries a golden
opportunity to initiate change, often with minimal resistance.
To use an analogy of the seasons, this governmental springtime
sees the sap rising and a flurry of activity. Ministerial optimism
abounds, although there are some aggrieved souls, who for
whatever reason have been ignored or passed over for ministerial
office. As ministers and their staff finally get to grips with priorities
and policies some form of summer arrives, green ministerial
shoots darken and on the surface at least there is a prospect of
purpose, progress and, in some quarters at least, popularity.

Occasional weather events disrupt matters in the form of setbacks, competition amongst ministries and the clash of egos. To outsiders and many of those within the Administration all appears well. With this collective sense that the Government is in rude health there is a greater unwillingness to question the Executive and slowly an atmosphere of cosy complacency begins to permeate the corridors of responsibility. Should a government begin to lose its way the summer soon begins to give way to that sense of satiation and ennui that is so redolent of early autumn. Ministers become detached and isolated and when dissenting voices are raised within the media or amongst societal stakeholders they constantly fulminate about their lot. Often a solid cadre of individuals seem unwilling or unable to recognise the dangers of the malaise that begins to envelope the Cabinet and before they realise it a political chill has set in that threatens governmental cohesion, policy and ultimately survival.

The issue of gender elucidates much about the existing prejudices that are prevalent in most legislative assemblies. Ministerial expectations tend to be viewed through a patriarchal prism and therefore skew the way in which policy priorities are shaped. Women aspiring to serve their country are already aware that they are likely to face many more obstacles across their path than their male counterparts, and there is also less likelihood that they will be called upon to hold the most prominent portfolios. In countries where women have achieved high office they find themselves exposed to unprecedented levels of personal scrutiny and criticism that tests their mental and physical resilience. Summers, in examining whether Australia's women political leaders are treated differently from men, is clear that this is a topic with real heat, one that in the course of her conversations with a number of past and present women political leaders reveal that: "The conversations are a somewhat sobering reminder that, despite the quite respectable number of women political leaders

Australia has now produced, our comfort level has not undergone a commensurate improvement." (Summers 2012)[65] According to Summers, preconceived notions of what a women should be continue to dominate the attitudes to women in politics and are particularly acute in regard of those who hold ministerial office: "You literally cannot win," says a cabinet minister. "You are criticised if you dedicate yourself to your career and don't have children. Or if you do have them, you're told you are neglecting your family. Or, when you spend time with them, that you are not doing your job properly." Julia Gillard, Prime Minister of Australia is on record as expressing her own concerns about the sexism and misogyny that she believes blights politics.

Figure 8: Women Members of Parliament around the World (2010)[66]

RWANDA	56.3%	1st
SWEDEN	54.4%	2nd
SOUTH AFRICA	44.5%	3rd
CUBA	44.3%	4th
ICELAND	42.9%	5th
UK	19.5%	73rd
USA	16.8%	91st
INDIA	10.8%	128th

Governments around the world have a woeful record on issues of gender based violence and whilst some Administrations go through the motions of addressing human wrongs, existing patriarchal mindsets frame ministries that have little interest in or desire to tackle injustice and violence with any understanding or zeal. The shamefully inept response of Ministers in India in regard to the gang rape and torture (and subsequent death) of young female physiotherapy intern in New Delhi 16th December 2012 speaks volumes of just how much work is needed when it comes to gender rights. Ministers were not only slow to respond, but lacking in empathy and understanding, as well as utterly incapable of comprehending public anger and concern. An understanding of crisis management and effective communication are integral to all organisations, and governments ignore this at their peril.

Gender is not the only issue here; there is also the attitude towards individuals living with disability as well as the fact that certain minority communities are underrepresented in or excluded from public office. Those in the public eye are under scrutiny as never before and it is more important than ever that they ensure that they are aware of the impact of their conduct and public and private utterances. Social networks such as Facebook, Twitter and YouTube, whilst making for potentially high impact campaigning vehicles, can be a double edged sword as they enable injudicious use to expose individuals to ridicule and censure. Some ministries have been slow to wake up to need for vigilance with regard to the personal, ministerial and governmental cyber footprint. Remaining mentally and physically alert is a key factor in political longevity.

Sensory alertness

A funambulist's ability to continue succeeding at their chosen profession relies to a very large extent on the ability to be attuned to minute changes. The ability to anticipate change as well as to adapt to what is going on around them can not only be the difference between success and failure, it could be the difference between life and death. All is not is always what it might seem, and the same is true of those who choose or are thrust into the political spotlight. All politicians must be alert to dangers, especially in their own political party; the harsh reality being that the world of politics is a world of dissemblers and deceivers, who speak the words of togetherness yet conspire to divide, exploit and betray.

In an increasingly cynical world there is an assumption that every politician and minister is out for themselves and that they take Niccolo Machiavelli's *The Prince* (1532) as their guidebook. Those setting out on their political journey would do well to remember that ultimately it is their own particular moral compass that will help them navigate the right path.

Political novices have their vocation tested frequently and if they fail to remain alert, potentially fall victim to the machinations and manipulations of others or are undone by their own complacency. High minded ideals and aspirations provide the motivation for many, whilst political horse-trading, vanity and venal self-interest are never far away. From the United Nations Headquarters in New York to Pacific islands there are examples of good and bad practice to warn and guide individuals who wish to serve their constituents and countries. An interesting case in point is the nation of Trinidad and Tobago, a country that on the surface may appear a paradise, but no amount of azure sky, crystal clear waters or sun-kissed beaches can hide the fact that these seemingly idyllic islands have witnessed dark clouds over paradise.

In the summer of 2011 following on from a concentrated spate of murders, some 11 in 48 hours[67], the President of Trinidad and Tobago issued a proclamation on Sunday 21st August 2011 declaring that a State of Emergency (SOE) had come into effect. For several days following on from this announcement there was considerable confusion as to whether it applied to the entire country or not and this confusion was added to by the fact that a subsequent Curfew Order was meant only to apply to specified "hot spots". As if a State of Emergency with a 9.00pm-5.00 am curfew were not serious enough, information subsequently emerged that elucidated something of the disorder that enveloped a decision supposedly meant to bring about order. At the point when the decision to act was taken, the Commissioner of Police

Dwaine Gibbs was in Brazil, something that came of a surprise to the Police Service Board (whom Commissioner Gibbs was required to notify if he intended to travel out of the country). Coincidently the Deputy Commissioner was also out of the country at the time. As for President George Maxwell Richards, he was presented with a *fait accompli* and had no choice but to 'sign' the State of Emergency which had already been put in place for 15 days (unless extended by Parliament) on the orders of Prime Minister Kamla Persad-Bissessar.

The exact reason for the action is still something for considerable conjecture. Drug smuggling, money laundering, gang culture and corruption at the highest levels have gnawed away the islands for years. The current government is adamant that the decision it took was for the good of all law-abiding citizens. The country's High Commissioner in London, Garvin Nicholas was robust in his defence of the decisions made by the People's Party Coalition, which since May 2010 has made up the Government in Port of Spain; "We are endeavouring to tackle a man-made disaster and we will employ all the necessary forces to deal with those criminal elements threatening our society." Nicholas was eager to make it clear where he believes the blame lies; ". . . our Government is determined to address the problems allowed to grow under the previous administration . . . we are committed to investing in the police, in youth recreation programmes and play areas and in tacking crime . . ." As a trained lawyer Nicholas played a straight bat and on the question of the criminality he stated; " . . . it is our intention to go after the minions of gang leaders, if you deal with them the gang leaders can no longer operate." Such sophistry seems somewhat at odds with the line taken by the Attorney General Anand Ramlogan, who made it clear that the "big fish"[68] were most definitely in the Government's sights.

Whilst the Government of Trinidad and Tobago may have wished to appear tough on crime there are those within its ranks who might not fully subscribe to its rhetoric. The sudden spike in killings was not the only reason why a State of Emergency was called. During the days and hours leading up to the decision, two shipping containers were unloaded and discovered at Port of Spain and these were found to be crammed with weapons and ammunition. Whilst being guarded by three police officers and five army personnel, one of the containers went missing. Senior military sources have confirmed that CCTV footage of the perpetrators of this crime was examined in the hunt to apprehend both the culprits and recapture the armaments. Such a brazen act, whilst bordering on the farcical, is a sinister reminder of the dark days of the previous State of Emergency in 1990 when there was an attempted coup.

The Prime Minister defended the draconian stance taken by her government and was defiant whilst speaking at a ceremony at Clifton Tower, Port of Spain:

> Make no mistake about it. This Government will remove lawlessness at every level from the society. It is time to bring discipline back, it is time to revive traditional values, and it is time to instil and even insist for rules and regulations, law and order. There is no room for compromise on this.[69]

For those at the very heart of Government such posturing was seriously undermined by a seeming moral malaise that was in danger of undermining the Administration at nearly every turn. The usually ebullient workaholic Austin "Jack" Warner—of FIFA fame, whilst keeping a somewhat lower profile during the crisis, remained firmly in control of the Ministry of Works and Infrastructure—a ministerial portfolio with the largest budget. Warner certainly wields enormous influence in Trinidad and Tobago and throughout the Caribbean and effectively bankrolled the United National Congress (the largest partner in the Coalition) in the two most recent elections and smoothed their path to victory in 2010.

If the Government was intent on rooting out lawlessness and had its heart set on some moral crusade, it would have needed to begin with those it selects to serve in positions of high office. For a country that has the dubious privilege of being a key route for the trans-shipment of narcotics, it does its reputation no good at all having Anil Roberts as Minister of Sport, an individual whose personal struggle to break his addition to cocaine has at times clouded his judgement to such an extent that he has believed that it is acceptable to use taxpayer funded government transport, including helicopters, to ferry his lover around. For all the fact the Government seeks to portray itself as a rainbow coalition, there is already bubbling discontent over the Indianisation of many of the ministries that has unpleasant shades of that which has caused so much tension in Guyana over the years. Whilst the Augean Stables remain uncleansed the earnest endeavours of elder statesmen such as Winston Dookeran will go largely unnoticed. Politicians are politicians and there will always be those who sadly fall well short of the ideal, just as Opposition parties will seek to make capital out of any government hitting a rough patch.

For the outside observer the events in Trinidad make for a fascinating study in how the political dynamic changes. With the State of Emergency now lifted, a degree of normality has returned. Jack Warner has now become Minister of National Security and Commissioner of Police Dwaine Gibbs has decided to take leave of his post early, leaving only an Acting Commissioner of Police and thus enhancing Warner's powers. All the signs are that the current Prime Minister wishes to become President in two years' time, thus avoiding the risk of losing a General Election and by so doing leaving the way open for Warner as the chief financial backer of the UNC Government to secure the Premiership should he wish so to do so. Even the dominant political forces in Trinidad and Tobago's do not have it all their own way with their Tobago surrogate the Tobago Organisation of the People (TOP) failing to win a single in the local election for the twelve seats in the Tobago House of Assembly on 21st January 2013.

Whilst there are countless examples of politicians who seek to profit from an artful manipulation of circumstances, there are others that rarely attract any real attention yet set about their duties with consummate professionalism. Those seeking to nurture such professionalism would do well to take inspiration from the sort of collaboration and cooperation that is a feature of biomimicry rather than Neo-Darwinism.

External Factors

When a Cabinet is being assembled a whole series of external factors have to be considered. In theory a cabinet should be made up of those best suited to individual portfolios, but in reality things are never that simple. Particular religious and ethnic groups may have to be considered, urban, peri-urban and rural constituencies, corporate players as well as party donors (whether these be from big business, unions or individuals), even occasionally external organisations such as key investors, major donors and the likes of the World Bank all have to be factored into the process. In some countries the military have enormous sway, whilst in others the media can exert tremendous pressure. Assembling a Cabinet is a veritable balancing act and that is before the egos, sensitivities and expectations of individuals are taken into account. One thing is for certain, and that is that decisions made will be criticised, egos bruised and enemies made both within and outside government.

Add to all this additional complications such as coalitions and wafer-thin majorities and the task becomes even more perilous and thwart with danger.

Ministers and those that aspire to ministerial office certainly require a pragmatic outlook and would do well to be stoical about their chances of affecting any real impact in the scheme of things. No sooner is an administration assembled then cracks begin to appear, even the redoubtable Margaret Thatcher (British Prime Minister 1979-1990) had members of her cabinet who she looked upon as 'wets' and therefore as at best weak and feeble, and at worse potentially disloyal. In India, the world's largest democracy, the national and state governments are constantly riven by internal dissention that undermines policy objectives. All of this is meat and drink to the media, who seem to delight in reporting such setbacks. Is it any wonder that ministers fear and cultivate the media in near equal measure? The sense of *schadenfreude* in media circles is often palpable and yet politicians themselves often make matters worse with off the record briefings and leaks. For all their reservations, no ministry can afford to ignore the power of the media. In countries such as India where literacy is improving all the time, headlines such as *BJP's tour plans go awry, thanks to rift*[70], and *Railway plans for Singur land to go awry*[71] are relatively tame. Nearly every move is put under the microscope and there is no shortage of advice from editorials for the likes of Prime Minister Manmohan Singh:

> Cabinet reshuffles are responses to anti-incumbency situations and offer a mid-course correction. The fact that a reshuffle should happen so early indicates that there was something amiss in the exercise that Singh undertook in May 2009. Either ministers were making money or they do not take his message 'hit the ground running' seriously. Implicit in his statement that he plans to undertake a 'more expansive' reshuffle after the

Budget session ends in May, is the fact that this exercise is a stopgap one. Ministers who are unhappy with the portfolios they have got would spend their time lobbying for new ones, instead of concentrating on their jobs. This message will percolate to the bureaucracy, which with its weathercock instincts, will be reluctant to put its best foot forward. Thus, on the face of it, the first Cabinet reshuffle appears flawed.[72]

Media exposés of ministerial inertia and incompetence, cabinet splits and corruption invariably grab the headlines, causing occasional firestorms that cost individual ministers and even governments to fall from grace. Governments in turn have been known to turn on their supposed tormentors as organisations such as the Committee to Protect Journalists, Index on Censorship and Reporters without Borders can testify to.

Bulging in-trays and countless appointments mean that Ministers are heavily dependent on their staff and whatever information they manage to glean from the media. The increasingly parochial nature of some media outlets as highlighted by reports such as *Shrinking World: The decline of international reporting in the British Press*[73] are a timely reminder of the challenges faced by ministers and policy makers if they are to be better placed to make informed decisions. Not so many years ago those who entered the Foreign Ministries of countries such as Britain and France were expected to be cultured individuals destined to be the public face of their nations in various corners of the globe. Historically British and French diplomatic legations in the Middle East and North Africa were staffed by an elite who not only mastered Arabic as easily as they had Latin and Ancient Greek, but were just as likely to be autodidacts who in their spare time would teach themselves Farsi and Hebrew along with Arabic calligraphy. For all their patrician virtues, these remarkable individuals still managed to generalise about the Arabs, Jews and Iranians and looked upon the regions they worked in as a chessboard of which they were the sole arbiters.

This gilded world lasted until the 1950's when Arab nationalism wreaked havoc upon the policies formulated by the Foreign Office in London and Ministry of Foreign Affairs in Paris and was to see the gluttonous King Farouk toppled in Egypt and the nationalisation of the Suez Canal. London and Paris, along with the newly created state of Israel, endeavoured to engineer an emergency to act as a cover for military intervention only to find that their machinations earned the disapproval and censure of the United States of America and resulted in a humiliating climb down. The fall-out from the Suez Crisis (1956) was far reaching, bolstering Gamal Abdel Nasser, emboldening the Soviet Union to send tanks into Hungary and sowing the seeds of discontent and treachery that was to result in the murder of the benign King Faisal II of Iraq and his family in 1958. One of Nasser's disciples, Brigadier Sallah in September 1962 was to orchestrate and execute an Egyptian-backed coup in Yemen, thus ousting Muhammad al-Badr—the Yemeni King and Imam, whilst the following year Abdul Salam Aref, another friend and admirer of the Egyptian leader, carried out the violent overthrow of Prime Minister Qasim of Iraq, an event that ushered in the era of the Ba'ath Party which ultimately was to lead to the rule of Saddam Hussein.

In the fifty years or so that have elapsed since much has happened that should be a clarion call for foreign policy makers to return to their history books or at the very least spend a few hours in the company of Arab taxi drivers in cities such as Amman, Cairo and Nablus. In this age of austerity and uncertainty maybe foreign policy makers in London and Paris could put "leverage" and "synergy" to one side and drink in some of the knowledge, opinions and wisdom to be found away from official vehicles and the Euro-mediocrities that fill their diplomatic social scene.

A battered yellow Mercedes-Benz could prove to be an unlikely place of learning and the driver a refreshing commentator, guide, historian and observer of local and international politics. These 'seats' of learning and transportation would of course include certain features as standard; small cups of cardamom coffee, pungent cheroots and the sublime if rather doleful voice of the unofficial Patron Saint of Arab taxi drivers—Oum Kaltoum. So what might the not-so-bright young things from Europe's foreign ministries gain from such an experience? Well, one thing is for certain, they had better be familiar with the following: The Sykes-Picot Agreement (1916) and The Balfour Declaration (1917).

Arab taxi drivers delight in exploring what has shaped their region and have an excellent working knowledge of the West's games and game players. Such is their knowledge that the world's top business schools and multi-nationals should be hiring some of them to draw up PESTLE analyses to help companies seeking to interact with the region. The knowledge, both general and specific of some British diplomats and Foreign & Commonwealth Office staff sent to the region is at times distinctly sketchy. Many have never even heard about John Bagot Glubb let alone read any of the writing of the famed Glubb Pasha; his books most notably *Great Arab Conquests* should be required reading. Mention the likes of Aden, the Trucial States and Nuri as-Said and you are greeted with quizzical looks and blank stares.

The Arab peoples whilst disparate in nature possess a strong sense of history, one which ensures that they are only too well aware of former triumphs and past and present slights. Diplomacy in the West has largely ignored history, even recent history and therefore is placed at a real disadvantage when it comes to engagement, establishing a rapport and understanding the mindset of those one deals with. The Hashemites of Jordan are taught from birth of their historical association with the Holy city of Mecca and the role the House of Saud played in ousting them, equally they understand that they owe their current status not due to a popular mandate but to being installed by the British and the patronage of the Americans. Whilst the Arabs treasure their sense of the past and delight in conspiracy theories (the latter being a favourite past time) those seeking to represent the West seem to have overlooked so much and what is worse at times appear utterly ignorant of what has gone before.

If policy makers in London and Paris seem ill prepared the situation in Washington is even more parlous. The US has been used to running much of the region by proxy and sometimes gives the impression it has made minimal effort to appreciate the dynamics and antipathies that shape inter-Arab rivalry or make the Arab League so utterly ineffective. America's foreign policy myopia has resulted in a siege mentality made worse by its total pre-occupation with Israel and Iran. Policy makers have bought into their own rhetoric and have routinely formulated solutions which bare little or no reality to the situation on the ground. This has been exacerbated by security concerns which have resulted in American diplomats being ever more detached and hamstrung. Recent events from the Maghreb and Mali to Damascus and the Persian Gulf have left Western diplomats dazed and confused. The morally dubious drone wars speak volumes of the paucity of creative thinking in the Corridors of Responsibility. The time is right for diplomats and those advising ministers and shaping policy to venture forth from their hermetically sealed offices and official cars and discover the real world again.

Predecessors, Contemporaries and Successors

Ministerial training such as it exists tends to be that which takes the form of heuristic learning. Established protocols and conventions shape the way post holders are expected to operate and those that stray too far from the norm risk being labelled unconventional, off-message and possibly disloyal and even dangerous. Societies that have been through periods of prolonged turmoil, particularly civil war, face a herculean task when it comes to re-establishing appropriate norms by which to operate efficiently and effectively. The polarisation of a nation whether on ethnic, religious or ideological grounds invariably corrodes the body politic and contorts the understanding of what public service means. Kumar talks of the immense challenge in bridging the "deep political cleavages between the warring factions" (Kumar: 1997: 4-5)[74] and goes on to identify the greatest failing: "An intrastate conflict indicates that the state has failed to govern itself—that is, to meet the essential needs and aspirations of its people and to effectively accommodate and reconcile the demands of competing groups within the framework of economic growth and political stability."[75] This analysis is a reminder to all governments and the ministers and ministries that comprise them that their *reason d'être* is about the aspirations of the people and the constant quest to balance expectations and priorities along with the internal and external dynamic. In examining the challenges faced by societies emerging from civil war, Kumar identifies three essential shortages; firstly the "decay of existing educational and training institutions and facilities"[76] which results in a critical shortage of trained and suitable personnel. Secondly, the fact that governments often labour under bloated bureaucracies that "inherit a plethora of superfluous departments, agencies and parastatal organisations"[77] and thirdly; "widespread inefficiency and a conspicuous lack of transparency"[78] These three shortages could well serve as a warning to all governments, for unless these areas are at the forefront of a Government's mind it too could fall victim to internal dissention that leads to the erosion of public trust that not only results in electoral defeat, but in extreme cases can result civil war.

There will always be examples of ministers and ministries that abuse power. That said, not all ministries are like those of the Ministry of Information and Publicity in Zimbabwe which in the year 2000 was both complicit in and an organiser of *Operation Tsuro*[79]—an act of systematic and state sponsored terror. Ministers and potential ministers-in-waiting are eager to make their mark and will use the legacy of their predecessors as a benchmark by which to gauge their own success. Those training and guiding ministers have a duty to make them aware that they are just as susceptible to endogenous and exogenous variables as anyone else. Like the funambulist they have to be aware of what has gone before, but equally what may lie ahead.

Each country's experience suggests that vibrant and robust political parties are crucial actors in articulating and aggregating diverse interests, providing visionary political leadership, recruiting and presenting candidates, and developing competing political and policy programmes upon which the electorate base their choices during elections.[80]

Ministers will be judged not only by their predecessors, by the conduct of their peers and by the record of those who come after them. Opposition parties and the media will always home in on examples of indolence, a tenuous grasp of the ministerial brief, or the appointment of personal friends as well as remunerated ministerial advisors. Peer pressure exists just as much in ministerial circles as it does in secondary schools. Ministers that fail to measure up at the despatch box or during press interviews must expect to be lampooned and ridiculed. Whilst the measuring of ministerial operational performance will always appear arbitrary, the standing of contemporaries and predecessors may well play a key role in deciding a minister's longevity in office. So many factors shape that elusive thing called success that it is beholden on all would-be ministers to give as much thought to their time out of office as on aiming to attain office. The challenges are seemingly endless. How many ministers-in-waiting have given thought to how their spouse or partner would handle questions from the media? What is it like to be mercilessly parodied in the press or have colleagues brief against you in times of crisis? Andragogy can be notoriously difficult at the best of times, but when it comes to being part of a government, quite simply there is a need to be ready for anything. Hamid Rashid Mohamed is candid in his acknowledgement of the fact that both he and his contemporaries that he first served with in Tanzania had had very little direct ministerial experience:

> Most of our leaders during our time were from the Liberation Parties or movements hence the ministers were mostly drawn from their political commitment to the liberation. Even though some had a good education, were honest, and possessed skills they had had very little exposure or experience of ministerial positions. They were Comrades in Arms. (see Appendix 1)

In seeking to help prepare a minister for public service it is important to remember that expectations have changed and what might have been tolerated in an earlier age will now no longer be tolerated. Citizens are increasingly adept at monitoring and exposing the misdeeds of those who hold public office. The proliferation of websites such as www.ipaidabribe.com (India) and comparable sites that focus on corruption in Kenya, Nigeria and Zimbabwe are helping empower citizens and change attitudes. The handing out of substantial fines and penalties to the likes of Oxford University Press East Africa (OUPEA)[81] also reminds us that the cancer of corruption has to be approached from various angles. Accountability and Transparency are the watchwords of sound ministerial leadership and whilst commercial interests will often be allowed to ride roughshod over the concerns of local people i.e.

over developments such as the Lamu Port South Sudan Ethiopia Transport Corridor (Lapsset)[82], citizens are increasingly demanding that their voice be heard.

There will always be people who wish to rail against ministers and ministries and, what is more, seek to tar all of those who hold public office with the same brush. Not all ministers are venal and a large number genuinely do empathise with their constituents and fellow citizens. Those willing to look for signs of positive change need look no further than President Joyce Banda of Malawi. On 7th June 2012, within weeks of her being elected President, Banda visited London and whilst there was invited to address a select gathering at Claridges. Having arrived late due to a miscommunication[83] she addressed the audience thus; "My protocol advisors inform me that Presidents and Prime Ministers never have to apologise. Well I do apologise. I have kept you waiting and I hope that you will forgive me for not having arrived on time." The affect of such an apology on the author and other members of the audience was quite remarkable.

Whilst circumstances vary enormously from state to state, ministers attest to the fact that they share common challenges. To simply expect them to deliver is both unkind and unreasonable. Training, guidance, mentoring and appraisal are invariably welcomed by ministers and would-be ministers, but sadly is in desperately short supply. Legislative Leaders increasingly recognize that the demands of the role they have embarked on means that they feel ill equipped and daunted by what lies before them. The tightrope walker at least mentally and physically prepares for the dangers he or she might face, but it is not until they are confronted with them that they are fully tested. A quotation variously attributed to two first ladies of the United States of America (Eleanor Roosevelt and Nancy Reagan) illustrates the point: A woman is like a tea bag, you cannot tell how strong she is until you put her in hot water—the same could equally be said of a government minister.

Funambulists appreciate the importance of balance in enabling them to achieve their objective. Governments and Legislative mechanisms must now seek to address the issue of balance—for too long we have heard about the corridors of power, it is now time to help prepare those appointed to serve for the corridors of responsibility. Ministers are not miracle workers, yet ministries in the right hands and with the appropriate support and training can perform near miraculous things against the odds.

PART 3

Conclusion

By Aliar Hossain

This book has sought to convey the range of factors that require careful consideration when addressing the immensely important, but hitherto neglected, concept of the ministerial mindset. It can be seen that what it encompasses strays onto such a variety of subjects and disciplines, that only through judgement and conscientiousness can ministers achieve the potential to which their position elevates them. It is perhaps this word judgement, fallen into relative disrepute, which provides the key to all the issues that lie before us. The incongruence of judgement in the modern age results from the fact that it cannot be assessed by grades and cannot shout over the clamour of voices or the rush for money. It combines elements that may be collected under terms such as wisdom, forethought, learning, inactivity, an openness to alternative thought in deed as well as in lip-service, hard work, discipline, rigour of assessment and so forth. If one seeks to reassert a faith in judgement, however, it cannot be conspicuously retained, if at all, only at the highest echelons. It must flow through every level of an organisation's functions—in the people and the practices, from the front door through to the extended hand of service.

This is the goal, but it can only be achieved by leadership. What is it then that ministers seek to achieve? How do they perceive the seal of their office? And how do they perceive it and continue to perceive it once they have stepped through its doors? This is the matter of the ministerial mindset.

Who enters the doors of office depends on a range of circumstances that cover the scope of social, political, economic and cultural characteristics that may differ from one country to the next. But arranging structures so that conscientious people will seek to enter, bringing with them a variety of skills, experience and achievements from the wider world, is one way to fast track improvement. It will help to bring the right people to the fore, such an elemental aspect of good governance. For whatever the structures, the work of government is affected by the qualities of the individuals involved—their judgement, social qualities, knowledge and the like. And this effect is contained not only for the duration of that individual's tenure, but spreads from him or her, and is communicated and nurtured in others as a real legacy. Whether such a legacy is for good or for ill, only structures, judgement and training can determine.

A programme of training can provide a first step to achieving a requisite level of capability and awareness amongst a greater number of government ministers. Training is a necessary compromise, designed to recognise and accommodate both the time pressures on incoming ministers and the unavoidable challenges that they will face. By instituting a flexible yet mandatory system, according to globally recognised standards, it is possible for sovereign states to overcome some of the most common recurring difficulties which ministers past and present have identified. Of all the requirements necessary to reaching a ministerial mindset, a programme of training is the most readily achievable. In most other avenues of employment, training has been recognised as a fundamental tool in improving performance. The failure to extend this to the political world is an anomaly and one whose obstinacy will rapidly dissipate upon the introduction of a well-crafted and comprehensive programme from above.

So beyond a programme of training tailored to meet the individual needs of the national government, the department and the minister, is it possible to take a deeper plunge, to look beyond current practice and current thinking and to join up the dots of our increasingly, rapidly interconnected world? I would argue that now is the moment to retrain our thinking and to readjust our horizons. Pioneering proposals are often met with doubt, resistance and apathy, but they are nevertheless worthwhile, nay necessary, for prising open new ways of thinking and mechanisms for future action. Given the new landscape of international relations, and of the international community itself, only bold new approaches to the subject can offer an effective future engagement.

What then is it that must be the defining technical goal in the creation of a ministerial mindset given the conditions of increased economic globalisation, the spread of universalistic conceptions of human rights, greater ease of communications, and population mobility? This goes to the heart of the competing notions regarding the sphere of power; in the context of the sovereign state: local or national; in the context of the international community: national or international. Whichever direction is taken in the future, and there will undoubtedly be inconsistencies and variation, international standards and mechanisms of censure will play an increasingly familiar role. Presently these are contained through multilateral institutions and, at its extreme point, through internationally sanctioned invasions and criminal court procedures. But it is likely that as the years, technology and economic integration advance, so will the complexity and reflexiveness of the mechanisms to support this. In this light, how can a ministerial mindset be crafted and nurtured for the benefit of succeeding generations?

It is proposed that ministers from across the globe should convene and have direct interaction with one another, for the purposes of seeking to improve institutional development and the effectiveness of their profession. This should be undertaken under the purview of the United Nations, transparently and without political bias—adapted to maintain principles such as those championed by Transparency International. As an independent body, funded by developed nations who recognise the benefits of increasing good governance across the globe, and monitored and moderated with the support of the leading universities and experts, it will be charged with producing an annual report assessing cabinet ministers and their activities across the world, distributed and made public to all. The immediate response one can detect will be as follows: no sovereign government will submit to independent analysis of their highly political, and in some cases corrupt and ineffective, activities. Nonetheless, the International Monetary Fund regularly produces reports as to the status of national economies, with its own interpretations of current statistics and future prospects, often at the cost of political embarrassment to the government in question. Its function is rarely questioned, though perhaps it findings may be disputed at times. By its very existence, by its regular and institutionalised fact, it is part of the landscape of the international community. As with a ministerial programme tailored and imposed as a fact within the national setting, its very existence provides its own justification and cause for acknowledgement.

The report should aim to set out key indicators such as corruption, the scope of representation, transparency of information, effectiveness and value for money—and provide measurements on an annual basis. It should also summarise fundamental features and developments over the course of the year, in terms of policies and ministerial engagements, and in terms of progress made according to the key indicators. From these first steps, can ministers, governments, civil servants, policymakers, academics, professional experts, and the domestic and international public be given the means to participate in an integrated debate and on a platform that embodies the international community. In time it will provide a historical record and foundation upon which developments or their lack can be assessed and identified.

This United Nations-led body should convene a forum once every year, bringing together ministers from all the countries of the world so that they are able to sit down and share their experiences. This is a forum not with regard to policy or national interest, but to benefiting their profession and improving the service they provide to their citizens. It will provide a space for ministers, both weak and strong, to learn from each other and to spread successful techniques, approaches and valuable training from which they may have benefited. The forum will also offer ministers the opportunity to participate in a range of workshops that seek to supplement their training and to build upon the discussions taking place. The defining aspect of this setting, the mindset that such a forum promotes, is one of professionalism, by which it is meant developing an understanding, amongst ministers and the wider public, that their role requires a set of qualities and knowledge upon which they can better deliver results.

Apart from generating a wider acknowledgement of the professional aspect of their undertaking, it should also create a mindset that the eye of the world is upon them. As in all professions, this is a fundamental aspect of good governance. Many ministers, especially in countries where civil society is weak, believe they are almighty and that there are few who can act against their intentions. Creating a global setting whereby the eye of censure is upon ministers will encourage a culture of good people—those who are conscientious, willing to accept criticism, be open to alternative opinions and seek to work in the common good—to enter politics. Because politics is not a game, a get rich quick scheme, or a sop to personal egos—it is a profession that should be designed not only to serve the people and meet their interests, but also to create the conditions under which society and the planet on which it relies, can flourish. We see this in the flow of the Ganges—it is not a zero-sum game of partition. By forging the conditions, one can create new supply and demand, and foster the circumstances for good living. Without the people with the vision, awareness and conscience to achieve this, it is not the share of resources that is affected, but the total availability. A ministerial mindset is a concept that requires judgement, knowledge, training, and management as well as social skills. It is not a specialisation, but it can benefit from it, whether this be in the form of expertise in a particular business or social sector, or in academic knowledge. A global institution under the auspices of the United Nations can help to create the conditions in which good people come into politics, ending a state of affairs whereby they are currently persuaded or forced away by the corruption of narrow power interests. Creating a ministerial mindset is about creating a culture, which can be achieved only slowly, but deliberately, through the building of international institutions and national frameworks to support ministerial training and the conditions to enable the best of the coming generations to serve on the global and regional stage.

Here then one must ask, is it important to attract a high quality of government minister, in all countries? And the answer must be yes. For all the undoubted benefits of economic growth generated from below, and of the centuries of development necessary for the build up of a public body and strong civil society institutions, direction from above affects the future health and well being of society. And again, in referring to society, one must talk about all that is encapsulated in it and about all upon which it rests. We talk here about freedom of thought and expression, and of strong networks of communication, in both directions, and in the multiple directions that will be bequeathed to us by future technology. Regulation, the rule of law, corruption, policies affecting the ecological basis of society and beyond are all at the mercy of decision-making and leadership undertaken by the government minister. This requires a responsibility to the citizens that the minister serves, but also a responsibility to the ministerial position itself. This means that a minister must be open to dialogue and welcome a wide range of opinions. But it also means taking responsibility, not abdicating decision-making under the sway of financially interested parties. This emphasis on being strong and yet open is not a contradiction, but an element of judgement. And it reinforces the need to prioritise values of judgement over inferior measurements. Here then one can see that it is only through judgement that one can fashion an appropriate ministerial mindset that incorporates within it a range of institutional supports as indicated above.

The structures of the international community, of the engagement between sovereign states and global citizens, is currently undergoing a transformation as great as any in the last few hundred years. Alongside this, the spread and development of knowledge, skills, techniques and ideas is following at a faster pace than at any other time in human history. To achieve good governance in the future requires not only an acknowledgement of these facts, but the embrace of these circumstances, which are welcome and offer new opportunities. By creating in theory, and working towards it in practice, a ministerial mindset with a global view, based upon what we need from ministers, we have an ambitious and yet possible new approach to dealing with the affairs of governance.

Bibliography

Alexander, D., Considine, M. and Lewis, J. (2012) *How Governments Think: The Role of Expertise, Cognitive Style, Creativity and Emotion in Public Policy and Management*, Public Management Research Conference: Seeking Excellence in a Time of Change, Fudan University, Shanghai, China, 25-27 May. Available at: http://www.sirpa.fudan.edu.cn/picture/article/122/cb/d6/c2b4ac86406488e07216f801c704/d4b55e8c-468a-474d-9e25-73f76a4d11be.pdf [Accessed: 22 September 2012].

Anolue, K. (2012) "Time to Change", *Nigerian Watch*, October.

BBC News (2011) Teacher Mohamed Ibrahim quits for Somalia deputy job, *BBC* [online], 9 September. Available at: http://www.bbc.co.uk/news/uk-england-london-14853043 (accessed 4 October 2012)

Beckman, Ludvig (2006) 'The Competent Cabinet? Ministers in Sweden and the Problem of Competence and Democracy', *Scandinavian Political Studies*, 29 (2), pp. 111-129. Available at: http://onlinelibrary.wiley.com/doi/10.1111/j.1467-9477.2006.00145.x/abstract [Accessed: 20 September 2012].

Biswas, A.K., Nakayama, M. and Uitto, J.I. (1998) *Standing in line for water: Cooperation on the Ganges and Brahmaputra*, The United Nations University. Available at: http://www.greenstone.org/greenstone3/nzdl;jses

sionid=8ECDB40223292D4A101B7F6532EA610A?a=d&c=ccgi&d=HASH
21d83324bab2981d08a266.3.np&sib=1&p.s=ClassifierBrowse&p.sa=&p.
a=b [Accessed: 24 November 2012].

Blair, T. (2010) *A Journey*, London: Hutchinson.

Blunden, M. (2012) Geopolitics and the Northern Sea Route, *International Affairs*, 88(1), pp. 115-129.

Bowlby, C. (2010) Can you teach cabinet ministers how to govern?, *BBC News*, 25 September. Available at: http://www.bbc.co.uk/news/uk-politics-11393714 [Accessed: 22 September 2012].

Business India (2011) "Post-reshuffle remedies", *Business India*, February.

Caribbean 360 (2011) 'Big fish' being targeted in state of emergency, *Caribbean 360* [online], 26 August. Available at: http://www.caribbean360.com/mobile/http://www.caribbean360.com/index.php/news/trinidad_tobago_news/499328.html (accessed 26 August 2011)

Caroselli, M. (2003) *Interpersonal Skills*, South Western/Thompson Learning.

Chanda, E. and Mwanza, T. (2012) Sata mocks inexperienced politicians, *The Post Newspapers*, 11 July. Available at: http://www.postzambia.com/post-print_article.php?articleId=28575 (accessed 10 October 2012)

Chikaya-Banda, J. (2012) *Duty of Care—Constitutional and law reform in Malawi*, Africa Research Institute.

Dale, I. (2009) In conversation with . . . . Jacqui Smith, *Total Politics*, 17 July. Available at: http://www.totalpolitics.com/articles/2463/in-conversation-with-jacqui-smith.thtml [Accessed: 22 September 2012].

Dempsey, J. (2011) Chinese Leader's Visit to Germany Ends with Large Trade Deals, *The New York Times* [online], 28 June. Available at: http://www.nytimes.com/2011/06/29/business/global/29wen.html?_r=0 [Accessed: 22 December 2012].

Earth Policy Institute (2006) *Data Indicators*. Available at: http://www.earth-policy.org/ [Accessed: 23 November 2012].

Emmerson, C. (2010) *The Future History of the Arctic*, London: The Bodley Head.

ENS Economic Bureau, (2012) Railway plans for Singur land goes awry, *The Indian Express* [online], 23 June. Available at: http://www.indianexpress.com/news/railway-plans-for-singur-land-to-go-awry/965632 (accessed 15 October 2012)

German-Foreign-Policy.com (2008) *Ice Cold War*, 11 June. Available at: http://www.german-foreign-policy.com/en/fulltext/56163 [Accessed: 22 December 2012].

Gruhn, Z. (2010) *Taking the Helm: Thoughts for Secretaries of State taking over a Department*, London: Institute for Government. Available at http://www.instituteforgovernment.org.uk/sites/default/files/Taking_the_Helm.pdf [Accessed: 23 September 2012].

Harper, M. (2012) *Joyce Banda at Claridge's*, [blog], 7 June. Available at: http://mary-harper.blogspot.co.uk/2012/06/joyce-banda-at-claridges.html (accessed 7 June 2012)

Hasan, Y.M. (2012) Somaliland: Government Prioritizes 2013-2014 Development Sectors, *Somaliland Sun* [online], 9 October. Available at: http://somalilandsun.com/index.php/politics/government/1608-somaliland-government-prioritizes-213-2014-development-sectors (accessed 15 October 2012)

Heseltine, M. (2001) *Life in the Jungle: My Autobiography*, London: Coronet.

Horn of Africa Business Association (2012) *Environmental fears as Port Lamu Development project is given the green light*, 6 March. Available at: http://ha-ba.com/environmental-fears-as-lamu-port-development-project-is-given-green-light/ (assessed 6 March 2012)

Horn of Africa Business Association (2012) *OUP receives a black mark from the World Bank*, 8 July. Available at: http://ha-ba.com/oxford-university-press-receives-a-black-mark-from-the-world-bank/ (accessed 8 July 2012)

House of Commons Public Administration Select Committee (2007) *Politics and Administration: Ministers and Civil Servants*, Third Report of Session 2006-2007, Volume I, HC 122-I, 26 March. Available at: http://www.publications.parliament.uk/pa/cm200607/cmselect/cmpubadm/122/122i.pdf [Accessed: 23 September 2012]

Humantrafficiking.org (2004) *First Coordinated Mekong Ministerial Initiative Against Trafficking (COMMIT) Senior Officials Meeting*, online], August. Available at: http://www.humantrafficking.org/updates/172 (accessed 4 October 2012)

Institute of Security Studies (2008) *Sierra Leone—A country review of crime and criminal justice.*

Inter-Parliamentary Union (2012) Women in Parliament. Available at: http://www.ipu.org/wmn-e/classif.htm (accessed 12th January 2012)

Johnston, P. (2007) The end of ministerial responsibility, *The Telegraph* [online], 17 September. Available at: http://www.telegraph.co.uk/comment/personal-view/3642739/The-end-of-ministerial-responsibility.html (accessed 26 September 2012)

Jyllands, P. (2012) Ministers lack real-world experience, *The Copenhagen Post*, 21 September. Available at: http://cphpost.dk/news/politics/ministers-lack-real-world-experience (accessed 25 September 2012)

Khalequzzaman, M. (2009) Tipaimukh Dam: Blessing or peril for Bangladesh?, *The Daily Star* [online], 12 July. Available at: http://www.thedailystar.net/newDesign/news-details.php?nid=96458 [Accessed: 27 November 2012].

Kumar, K. (ed.) (1997) *Rebuilding Societies after Civil War*. Lyne Rienner Publishers Inc.

Mirza, M.M.Q. (1997) Hydrological changes in the Ganges system in Bangladesh in the post-Farakka period, *Hydrological Sciences Journal*, 42(5), pp. 613-631. Available at: http://www.iahs.info/hsj/420/hysj_42_05_0613.pdf [Accessed: 26 November 2012].

Mollinga, P.P. (2008) Water, Politics and Development: Framing a Political Sociology of Water Resources Management, *Water Alternatives*, 1(1), pp. 7-23. Available at: http://www.ibcperu.org/doc/isis/8847.pdf [Accessed: 10 December 2012].

Moore, M. (2010) *Shrinking World: The decline of international reporting in the British Press*, Media Standards Trust.

Neaves, J. (2011) Kamla: we'll take them out in one way or another, *Trinidad Express Newspapers* [online], 27 August. Available at: http://www.trinidadexpress.com/news/Kamla__We_ll_take_them_out_in_one_way_or_another-128515553.html (accessed 27 August 2011)

Nonaka, J., Toyama, R., Konno, N., SECI, Ba and Leadership: a Unified Model of the Dynamic Knowledge Creation, Long Range Planning, 2000, No 33

Norton, Philip (Lord Norton of Louth) (1999) 'How to be a minister—Get some training!' *The Edge—The ESCR Policy Forum for Executive Action*, 1, May, pp. 4. Available at: http://www.esrc.ac.uk/_images/ The%20Edge%201_tcm8-8208.pdf [Accessed: 22 September 2012].

Payne, A.I., Sinha, R., Singh, H.R. and Huq, S. (2004) 'A Review of the Ganges Basin: Its Fish and Fisheries', in Welcomme, R.L. and Peter, T. (eds.) *Proceedings of the Second International Symposium on the Management of Large Rivers for Fisheries: Volume I*, Sustaining Livelihoods and Biodiversity in the New Millennium, 11-14 February 2003, Phnom Penh, Bangkok: Food and Agriculture Organization of the United Nations and The Mekong River Commission, 2004/16, pp. 229-251. Available at: http://www.apfic.org/apfic_downloads/pubs_RAP/2004-16.pdf#page=243 [Accessed: 26 November 2012].

Public Administration Select Committee (2007) *Skills for Government*, Report of the 2006-07 session. Available at www.publications.parliament. uk/pa/cm200607/cmselect/cmpubadm/93/9302.htm [Accessed: 23 September 2012].

Public Administration Select Committee (2011) *Smaller Government: What do Ministers do?*, Seventh Report of Session 2010-11. Available at http://www. publications.parliament.uk/pa/cm201011/cmselect/cmpubadm/530/530. pdf [Accessed:[84] 23 September 2012].

Richards, P. (2011) Limited State of Emergency declared in Trinidad and Tobago, Caricom News Network [online], 22 August. Available at: http:// caricomnewsnetwork.com/index.php?option=com_content&view=article &id=4939:trinidad-limited-state-of-emergency-declared-in-trinidad-and-tobago&catid=54:latest-news (accessed 26 August 2011)

Riddell, P., Gruhn, Z. and Carolan, L. (2011) *The Challenge of Being a Minister: Defining and Developing Ministerial Effectiveness*, London: Institute for Government. Available at: http://www.instituteforgovernment.

org.uk/sites/default/files/publications/The%20Challenge%20of%20 Being%20a%20Minister.pdf [Accessed: 22 September 2012].

Riddell, P. and Haddon, C. (2011) *Transitions: Lessons Learned*, London: Institute for Government, pp. 17-22. Available at: http://www. instituteforgovernment.org.uk/publications/transitions-lessons-learned [Accessed: 23 September 2012].

Sachikonye, L. (2011) *When a State turns on its Citizens*. Jacana Media Ltd.

Siddiqi, A. (2011) Kashmir and the politics of water, *aljazeera.com* [online], 1 August. Available at: http://www.aljazeera.com/indepth/spotlight/kash mirtheforgottenconflict/2011/07/20117812154478992.html [Accessed: 29 November 2012].

SIPRI (2012) *Military expenditure as a share of GDP, 2005-2010*, Stockholm International Peace Research Institute. Available at: http://www.sipri.org/ research/armaments/milex/resultoutput/milex_gdp (accessed 14 October 2012)

Somolekae, G. (2006) *Political Parties in Botswana*. EISA.

Steinberg, P.E. and Clark, G.E. (1999) Troubled Water? Acquiescence, conflict, and the politics of place in watershed management, *Political Geography*, 18, pp. 477-508. Available at: http://mailer.fsu.edu/~psteinbe/ garnet-psteinbe/polgeogwach.pdf [Accessed: 10 December 2012].

Sonntag, M. and Luth, F. (2011) Who Owns the Arctic? A Stocktaking of Territorial Disputes, *The Global Journal* [online], 11 December. Available at: http://theglobaljournal.net/article/view/439/ [Accessed: 14 December 2012].

Summers, A. (2012) The gender agenda: Gillard and the politics of sexism, *National Times* [online], 26 February. Available at: http://www.smh.com.

au/opinion/political-news/the-gender-agenda-gillard-and-the-politics-of-sexism-20120225-1tv7n.html (accessed 24 October 2012)

The Times of India (2012) BJP's tour plans go awry thanks to rift, *The Times of India* [online], 21 August. Available at: http://articles.timesofindia. indiatimes.com/2012-08-21/bangalore/33301931_1_bjp-state-president-bjp-national-general-secretary-bjp-in-poll-mode (accessed 15 October 2012)

The World Bank (2010) *Shipbreaking and Recycling Industry in Bangladesh and Pakistan*. Report number 58275-SAS.

Tiernan, A. and Weller, P. (2010) *Learning to be a Minister: Heroic Expectations, Practical Realities*, Melbourne: Melbourne University Press.

Walker, J. (2010) *Training for MPs and ministers*, Whatdotheyknow.org [online], June. Available at: http://www.whatdotheyknow.com/request/training_for_mps_and_ministers?unfold=1 (accessed 8 October 2012)

Webster, A. (2009) The benefits of ministerial continuity, *The Spectator*, 16 July. Available at http://blogs.spectator.co.uk/coffeehouse/2009/07/the-benefits-of-ministerial-continuity/ [Accessed: 22 September 2012].

Wolf, A.T. (2001) Water and Human Security, *Journal of Contemporary Water Research and Education*, 118(1), pp. 29-37. Available at: http://opensiuc.lib.siu.edu/jcwre/vol118/iss1/5/ [Accessed: 26 November 2012].

Wolf, A.T. and Newton, J.T. (2008) *Case Study of Transboundary Dispute Resolution: The Ganges River Controversy*, Institute for Water and Watersheds, Oregon State University. Available at: http://www.transboundarywaters.orst.edu/research/case_studies/Ganges_New.htm [Accessed: 27 November 2012].

Notes

1   Tiernan, A. and Weller, P. (2010) *Learning to be a Minister: Heroic Expectations, Practical Realities*, Melbourne: Melbourne University Press, p. x.

2   Dale, I. (2009) In conversation with . . . . Jacqui Smith, *Total Politics*, 17 July. Available at: http://www.totalpolitics.com/articles/2463/in-conversation-with-jacqui-smith.thtml [Accessed: 22 September 2012].

3   Webster, A. (2009) The benefits of ministerial continuity, *The Spectator*, 16 July. Available at http://blogs.spectator.co.uk/coffeehouse/2009/07/the-benefits-of-ministerial-continuity/ [Accessed: 22 September 2012].

4   Heseltine, M. (2001) *Life in the Jungle: My Autobiography*, London: Coronet.

5   Tiernan, A. and Weller, P. (2010) *Learning to be a Minister: Heroic Expectations, Practical Realities*, Melbourne: Melbourne University Press, p. 66.

6   Bowlby, C. (2010) Can you teach cabinet ministers how to govern?, *BBC News*, 25 September. Available at: http://www.bbc.co.uk/news/uk-politics-11393714 [Accessed: 22 September 2012].

7   Riddell, P., Gruhn, Z. and Carolan, L. (2011) *The Challenge of Being a Minister: Defining and Developing Ministerial Effectiveness*, London: Institute for Government, p. 15. Available at: http://www.instituteforgovernment.org.uk/sites/default/files/publications/The%20Challenge%20of%20Being%20a%20Minister.pdf [Accessed: 22 September 2012].

8   House of Commons Public Administration Select Committee (2007) *Politics and Administration: Ministers and Civil Servants*, Third Report of Session 2006-2007, Volume I, HC 122-I, 26 March, p. 9. Available

at: http://www.publications.parliament.uk/pa/cm200607/cmselect/cmpubadm/122/122i.pdf [Accessed: 23 September 2012]

9   Riddell, P., Gruhn, Z. and Carolan, L. (2011) *The Challenge of Being a Minister: Defining and Developing Ministerial Effectiveness*, London: Institute for Government, p. 43. Available at: http://www.instituteforgovernment.org.uk/sites/default/files/publications/The%20Challenge%20of%20Being%20a%20Minister.pdf [Accessed: 22 September 2012].

10 Riddell, P., Gruhn, Z. and Carolan, L. (2011) *The Challenge of Being a Minister: Defining and Developing Ministerial Effectiveness*, London: Institute for Government, p. 16. Available at: http://www.instituteforgovernment.org.uk/sites/default/files/publications/The%20Challenge%20of%20Being%20a%20Minister.pdf [Accessed: 22 September 2012].

11 Alexander, D., Considine, M. and Lewis, J. (2012) *How Governments Think: The Role of Expertise, Cognitive Style, Creativity and Emotion in Public Policy and Management*, Public Management Research Conference: Seeking Excellence in a Time of Change, Fudan University, Shanghai, China, 25-27 May, p. 20. Available at: http://www.sirpa.fudan.edu.cn/picture/article/122/cb/d6/c2b4ac86406488e07216f801c704/d4b55e8c-468a-474d-9e25-73f76a4d11be.pdf [Accessed: 22 September 2012].

12 Riddell, P., Gruhn, Z. and Carolan, L. (2011) *The Challenge of Being a Minister: Defining and Developing Ministerial Effectiveness*, London: Institute for Government, p. 14. Available at: http://www.instituteforgovernment.org.uk/sites/default/files/publications/The%20Challenge%20of%20Being%20a%20Minister.pdf [Accessed: 22 September 2012].

13 Public Administration Select Committee (2011) *Smaller Government: What do Ministers do?*, Seventh Report of Session 2010-11, p. 28. Available at http://www.publications.parliament.uk/pa/cm201011/cmselect/cmpubadm/530/530.pdf [Accessed: 23 September 2012].

14 Blair, T. (2010) *A Journey*, London: Hutchinson, p.1.

15 Riddell, P. and Haddon, C. (2011) *Transitions: Lessons Learned*, London: Institute for Government, pp. 17-22. Available at: http://www.instituteforgovernment.org.uk/publications/transitions-lessons-learned [Accessed: 23 September 2012].

16 Public Administration Select Committee (2007) *Skills for Government*, Report of the 2006-07 session, para. 146. Available at www.publications.

standing nationally and in the eyes of the Government and public. It often helps if ministers understand that national interest is not at odds with self-interest, the two are not mutually exclusive.

Mental and Physical State

Ministers become part of an organisation, one which is shaped by codes and norms. If an Administration is to survive and succeed for any length of time without recourse to repression of the populace it could gain much from examining the SECI Model, otherwise known as the knowledge spiral, a model developed by J. Nonaka, R. Toyama, and N. Konno. The SECI Model (SECI is an acronym of socialisation, externalisation, combination and internationalisation) distinguishes between explicit knowledge and tacit knowledge. In this model, four modes of knowledge conversion were identified:

1. Tacit to Tacit (Socialization)—This dimension explains Social interaction as tacit to tacit knowledge transfer, sharing tacit knowledge through face-to-face or sharing knowledge through experiences. For example, meetings and brainstorming can support this kind of interaction. Since tacit knowledge is difficult to formalize and often time and space specific, tacit knowledge can be acquired only through shared experience, such as spending time together or living in the same environment. Socialization typically occurs in a traditional apprenticeship, where apprentices learn the tacit knowledge needed in their craft through hands-on experience, rather than from written manuals or textbooks.

2. Tacit to Explicit (Externalization)—Between tacit and explicit knowledge by Externalization (publishing, articulating knowledge), developing factors, which embed the

parliament.uk/pa/cm200607/cmselect/cmpubadm/93/9302.htm [Accessed: 23 September 2012].

17   Riddell, P., Gruhn, Z. and Carolan, L. (2011) *The Challenge of Being a Minister: Defining and Developing Ministerial Effectiveness*, London: Institute for Government, p. 47. Available at: http://www.instituteforgovernment.org.uk/sites/default/files/publications/The%20Challenge%20of%20Being%20a%20Minister.pdf [Accessed: 22 September 2012].

18   Steinberg, P.E. and Clark, G.E. (1999) Troubled Water? Acquiescence, conflict, and the politics of place in watershed management, *Political Geography*, 18, p. 478. Available at: http://mailer.fsu.edu/~psteinbe/garnet-psteinbe/polgeogwach.pdf [Accessed: 10 December 2012].

19   Mollinga, P.P. (2008) Water, Politics and Development: Framing a Political Sociology of Water Resources Management, *Water Alternatives*, 1(1), pp. 7-23. Available at: http://www.ibcperu.org/doc/isis/8847.pdf [Accessed: 10 December 2012].

20   Mollinga, P.P. (2008) Water, Politics and Development: Framing a Political Sociology of Water Resources Management, *Water Alternatives*, 1(1), p. 7. Available at: http://www.ibcperu.org/doc/isis/8847.pdf [Accessed: 10 December 2012].

21   Mollinga, P.P. (2008) Water, Politics and Development: Framing a Political Sociology of Water Resources Management, *Water Alternatives*, 1(1), p. 12. Available at: http://www.ibcperu.org/doc/isis/8847.pdf [Accessed: 10 December 2012].

22   Siddiqi, A. (2011) Kashmir and the politics of water, *aljazeera.com* [online], 1 August. Available at: http://www.aljazeera.com/indepth/spotlight/kashmirtheforgottenconflict/2011/07/20117812154478992.html [Accessed: 29 November 2012].

23   Siddiqi, A. (2011) Kashmir and the politics of water, *aljazeera.com* [online], 1 August. Available at: http://www.aljazeera.com/indepth/spotlight/kashmirtheforgottenconflict/2011/07/20117812154478992.html [Accessed: 29 November 2012].

24   Earth Policy Institute (2006) *Data Indicators*. Available at: http://www.earth-policy.org/ [Accessed: 23 November 2012].

25   Biswas, A.K., Nakayama, M. and Uitto, J.I. (1998) *Standing in line for water: Cooperation on the Ganges and Brahmaputra*, The United Nations University. Available at: http://www.greenstone.org/greenstone3/nzdl;jsessionid=8ECDB40223292D4A101B7F6532EA610

A?a=d&c=ccgi&d=HASH21d83324bab2981d08a266.3.np&sib=1&p. s=ClassifierBrowse&p.sa=&p.a=b [Accessed: 24 November 2012].

26 Biswas, A.K., Nakayama, M. and Uitto, J.I. (1998) *Standing in line for water: Cooperation on the Ganges and Brahmaputra*, The United Nations University. Available at: http://www.greenstone.org/ greenstone3/nzdl;jsessionid=8ECDB40223292D4A101B7F6532EA610 A?a=d&c=ccgi&d=HASH21d83324bab2981d08a266.3.np&sib=1&p. s=ClassifierBrowse&p.sa=&p.a=b [Accessed: 24 November 2012].

27 Mirza, M.M.Q. (1997) Hydrological changes in the Ganges system in Bangladesh in the post-Farakka period, *Hydrological Sciences Journal*, 42(5), pp. 613-631. Available at: http://www.iahs.info/hsj/420/ hysj_42_05_0613.pdf [Accessed: 26 November 2012].

28 Mirza, M.M.Q. (1997) Hydrological changes in the Ganges system in Bangladesh in the post-Farakka period, *Hydrological Sciences Journal*, 42(5), pp. 613-631. Available at: http://www.iahs.info/hsj/420/ hysj_42_05_0613.pdf [Accessed: 26 November 2012].

29 Mirza, M.M.Q. (1997) Hydrological changes in the Ganges system in Bangladesh in the post-Farakka period, *Hydrological Sciences Journal*, 42(5), pp. 613-631. Available at: http://www.iahs.info/hsj/420/ hysj_42_05_0613.pdf [Accessed: 26 November 2012].

30 Payne, A.I., Sinha, R., Singh, H.R. and Huq, S. (2004) 'A Review of the Ganges Basin: Its Fish and Fisheries', in Welcomme, R.L. and Peter, T. (eds.) *Proceedings of the Second International Symposium on the Management of Large Rivers for Fisheries: Volume I*, Sustaining Livelihoods and Biodiversity in the New Millennium, 11-14 February 2003, Phnom Penh, Bangkok: Food and Agriculture Organization of the United Nations and The Mekong River Commission, 2004/16, pp. 229-251. Available at: http://www.apfic.org/apfic_downloads/ pubs_RAP/2004-16.pdf#page=243 [Accessed: 26 November 2012].

31 Wolf, A.T. (2001) Water and Human Security, *Journal of Contemporary Water Research and Education*, 118(1), p. 31. Available at: http:// opensiuc.lib.siu.edu/jcwre/vol118/iss1/5/ [Accessed: 26 November 2012].

32 Wolf, A.T. and Newton, J.T. (2008) *Case Study of Transboundary Dispute Resolution: The Ganges River Controversy*, Institute for Water and Watersheds, Oregon State University. Available at: http://www. transboundarywaters.orst.edu/research/case_studies/Ganges_New. htm [Accessed: 27 Novermber 2012].

33   Wolf, A.T. and Newton, J.T. (2008) *Case Study of Transboundary Dispute Resolution: The Ganges River Controversy*, Institute for Water and Watersheds, Oregon State University. Available at: http://www. transboundarywaters.orst.edu/research/case_studies/Ganges_New. htm [Accessed: 27 Novermber 2012].

34   Wolf, A.T. and Newton, J.T. (2008) *Case Study of Transboundary Dispute Resolution: The Ganges River Controversy*, Institute for Water and Watersheds, Oregon State University. Available at: http://www. transboundarywaters.orst.edu/research/case_studies/Ganges_New. htm [Accessed: 27 Novermber 2012].

35   Khalequzzaman, M. (2009) Tipaimukh Dam: Blessing or peril for Bangladesh?, *The Daily Star* [online], 12 July. Available at: http://www. thedailystar.net/newDesign/news-details.php?nid=96458 [Accessed: 27 November 2012].

36   Sonntag, M. and Luth, F. (2011) Who Owns the Arctic? A Stocktaking of Territorial Disputes, *The Global Journal* [online], 11 December. Available at: http://theglobaljournal.net/article/view/439/ [Accessed: 14 December 2012].

37   Sonntag, M. and Luth, F. (2011) Who Owns the Arctic? A Stocktaking of Territorial Disputes, *The Global Journal* [online], 11 December. Available at: http://theglobaljournal.net/article/view/439/ [Accessed: 14 December 2012].

38   Blunden, M. (2012) Geopolitics and the Northern Sea Route, *International Affairs*, 88(1), pp. 115-129.

39   Brigham, L.W. (2011) Russia opens its marine Arctic, *Proceedings of the US Naval Institute*, 137(5/1), p. 299, cited in Blunden, M. (2012) Geopolitics and the Northern Sea Route, *International Affairs*, 88(1), p. 116.

40   Brigham, L.W. (2011) Russia opens its marine Arctic, *Proceedings of the US Naval Institute*, 137(5/1), p. 299, cited in Blunden, M. (2012) Geopolitics and the Northern Sea Route, *International Affairs*, 88(1), p. 116.

41   Blunden, M. (2012) Geopolitics and the Northern Sea Route, *International Affairs*, 88(1), pp. 115-129.

42   Blunden, M. (2012) Geopolitics and the Northern Sea Route, *International Affairs*, 88(1), pp. 115-129.

43   Dempsey, J. (2011) Chinese Leader's Visit to Germany Ends with Large Trade Deals, *The New York Times* [online], 28 June. Available at: http://

www.nytimes.com/2011/06/29/business/global/29wen.html?_r=0 [Accessed: 22 December 2012].

[44] German-Foreign-Policy.com (2008) *Ice Cold War*, 11 June. Available at: http://www.german-foreign-policy.com/en/fulltext/56163 [Accessed: 22 December 2012].

[45] German-Foreign-Policy.com (2008) *Ice Cold War*, 11 June. Available at: http://www.german-foreign-policy.com/en/fulltext/56163 [Accessed: 22 December 2012].

[46] Caroselli, M. (2003) *Interpersonal Skills*, South Western/Thompson Learning

[47] Ibid

[48] Anolue, K. (2012) "Time to Change", *Nigerian Watch,* October 2012, p. 17.

[49] Hasan, Y.M. (2012) Somaliland: Government Prioritizes 2013-2014 Development Sectors, *Somaliland Sun* [online], 9 October. Available at: http://somalilandsun.com/index.php/politics/government/1608-somaliland-government-prioritizes-213-2014-development-sectors (accessed 15 October 2012)

[50] BBC News (2011) Teacher Mohamed Ibrahim quits for Somalia deputy job, *BBC* [online], 9 September. Available at: http://www.bbc.co.uk/news/uk-england-london-14853043 (accessed 4 October 2012)

[51] Walker, J. (2010) *Training for MPs and ministers*, Whatdotheyknow.org [online], June. Available at: http://www.whatdotheyknow.com/request/training_for_mps_and_ministers?unfold=1 (accessed 8 October 2012)

[52] Institute of Security Studies (2008) *Sierra Leone—A country review of crime and criminal justice.*

[53] Ibid

[54] Humantrafficiking.org (2004) *First Coordinated Mekong Ministerial Initiative Against Trafficking (COMMIT) Senior Officials Meeting,* online], August. Available at: http://www.humantrafficking.org/updates/172 (accessed 4 October 2012)

[55] Water—The missing ingredient in real and sustained economic development, Keynote Address delivered at the International Conference on Business & Economic Development, Las Vegas, 23 July 2012

[56] Jyllands, P. (2012) Ministers lack real-world experience, *The Copenhagen Post*, 21 September. Available at: http://cphpost.dk/news/politics/ministers-lack-real-world-experience (accessed 25 September 2012)

57   Ibid

58   Chanda, E. and Mwanza, T. (2012) Sata mocks inexperienced politicians, *The Post Newspapers*, 11 July. Available at: http://www.postzambia.com/post-print_article.php?articleId=28575 (accessed 10 October 2012)

59   Johnston, P. (2007) The end of ministerial responsibility, *The Telegraph* [online], 17 September. Available at: http://www.telegraph.co.uk/comment/personal-view/3642739/The-end-of-ministerial-responsibility.html (accessed 26 September 2012)

60   The World Bank (2010) Shipbreaking and Recycling Industry in Bangladesh and Pakistan. Report number 58275-SAS.

61   http://www.public-standards.gov.uk/About/The_7_Principles.html (accessed 10 October 2012)

62   Chikaya-Banda, J. (2012) *Duty of Care—Constitutional and law reform in Malawi*, Africa Research Institute.

63   SIPRI (2012) *Military expenditure as a share of GDP, 2005-2010*, Stockholm International Peace Research Institute. Available at: http://www.sipri.org/research/armaments/milex/resultoutput/milex_gdp (accessed 14 October 2012)

64   Nonaka, J., Toyama, R. and Konno, N. (2000) SECI, Ba and Leadership : a Unified Model of the Dynamic Knowledge Creation, Long Range Planning, No 33. Wikipedia (2013) SECI Model. Available at: http://en.wikipedia.org/wiki/File:SECI_Model.jpg (accessed 15 April 2013)

65   Summers, A. (2012) The gender agenda: Gillard and the politics of sexism, *National Times* [online], 26 February. Available at: http://www.smh.com.au/opinion/political-news/the-gender-agenda-gillard-and-the-politics-of-sexism-20120225-1tv7n.html (accessed 24 October 2012)

66   Inter-Parliamentary Union (2012) Women in Parliament. Available at: http://www.ipu.org/wmn-e/classif.htm (accessed 12th January 2012)

67   Richards, P. (2011) Limited State of Emergency declared in Trinidad and Tobago, Caricom News Network [online], 22 August. Available at: http://caricomnewsnetwork.com/index.php?option=com_content&view=article&id=4939:trinidad-limited-state-of-emergency-declared-in-trinidad-and-tobago&catid=54:latest-news (accessed 26 August 2011)

68   Caribbean 360 (2011) 'Big fish' being targeted in state of emergency, *Caribbean 360* [online], 26 August. Available at: http://www.

caribbean360.com/mobile/http://www.caribbean360.com/index.php/news/trinidad_tobago_news/499328.html (accessed 26 August 2011)

69 Neaves, J. (2011) Kamla: we'll takem them out in one way or another, *Trinidad Express Newspapers* [online], 27 August. Available at: http://www.trinidadexpress.com/news/Kamla__We_ll_take_them_out_in_one_way_or_another-128515553.html (accessed 27 August 2011)

70 The Times of India (2012) BJP's tour plans go awry thanks to rift, *The Times of India* [online], 21 August. Available at: http://articles.timesofindia.indiatimes.com/2012-08-21/bangalore/33301931_1_bjp-state-president-bjp-national-general-secretary-bjp-in-poll-mode (accessed 15 October 2012)

71 ENS Economic Bureau (2012) Railway plans for Singur land goes awry, *The Indian Express* [online], 23 June. Available at: http://www.indianexpress.com/news/railway-plans-for-singur-land-to-go-awry/965632 (accessed 15 October 2012)

72 "Post-reshuffle remedies", *Business India*, February 2011, p. 6.

73 Moore, M. (2010) *Shrinking World: The decline of international reporting in the British Press*, Media Standards Trust.

74 Kumar, K. (ed.) (1997). *Rebuilding Societies after Civil War.* Lyne Rienner Publishers Inc.

75 Ibid

76 Ibid

77 Ibid

78 Ibid

79 Sachikonye, L. (2011) *When a State turns on its Citizens.* Jacana Media Ltd.

80 Somolekae, G. (2006) *Political Parties in Botswana.* EISA.

81 Horn of Africa Business Association (2012) *OUP receives a black mark from the World Bank*, 8 July. Available at: http://ha-ba.com/oxford-university-press-receives-a-black-mark-from-the-world-bank/ (accessed 8 July 2012)

82 Horn of Africa Business Association (2012) *Environmental fears as Port Lamu Development project is given the green light*, 6 March. Available at: http://ha-ba.com/environmental-fears-as-lamu-port-development-project-is-given-green-light/ (assessed 6 March 2012)

83 Harper, M. (2012) *Joyce Banda at Claridge's*, [blog], 7 June. Available at: http://mary-harper.blogspot.co.uk/2012/06/joyce-banda-at-claridges.html (accessed 7 June 2012)

Appendix 1

An interview with Hamid Rashid Mohamed MP, who served as:

Deputy Minister of Home Affairs, United Republic Of Tanzania, 1982-1987

Deputy Minister of Finance and Economy Affairs, United Republic Of Tanzania, 1987-1988

He is no stranger to the dangers and vicissitudes of being a public servant, having been a Prisoner of Conscience in Zanzibar from 1997-2000 (Amnesty International successfully campaigned for his release). In recent years his public service has seen him occupy a series of significant roles:

Leader of Official Opposition and Shadow Minister of Finance and Economy, 2005-2010

Member of the Parliamentary Committee on Finance and Economic Affairs, 2005-2013

Member of the Parliamentary Standing Committee of IPU on Sustainable Development Finance and Trade, 2011-to date (Vice President representing the Geo Group of Africa)

Member of Parliamentary Service Commission of the United Republic Of Tanzania Parliament, 2005-2016

Member of APNAC (A parliamentarian organisation against Corruption), 2005-2015

1) What do you believe are the three most important skills required of a new government minister?

Every forest has its own creatures. Our times are very different, with the present much more globalised world. Today transparency is the key to any decision you make, whether it is an appointment, election or employment. It is a world of competition, hence even being in Cabinet has become very competitive.

Most of our leaders during our time were from the Liberation Parties or movements hence the ministers were mostly drawn from their political commitment to the liberation. Even though some had a good education, were honest, and possessed skills they had had very little exposure or experience of ministerial positions. They were Comrades in Arms.

Today a minister must have a good education, so as to read, listen, understand and communicate. An effective minister has to understand his or her constitutional and political constraints; along with their responsibilities to the appointing authority within the government, parliament, the media, the public and the constituency they represent.

Secondly, they should be ready to learn quickly from experience and stay focused on ministerial objectives.

Thirdly, they should be confident in themselves, be honest and should always strive to walk in the ways of truth. If they do this then God will bless them and people will respect them.

2) What motivated you to enter politics and how has your attitude to Public Service changed since becoming a minister?

My father was among the great politicians of his time, fighting for independence in the 1950s and 60s. His example greatly influenced me and my brothers and we became greatly interested in politics. I became very excited when he stood for election the first time, he lost by only 242 votes and I still recall I did not want to eat. I became politically active even at school and college. While at college and in work, I used to say that our great leaders had done their job in helping liberate the country, now it is our duty to bring about change to our people, a change built on hope and better economic and social development. The Nation needs us to play our part. That is why after working for 7 years in a bank (People's Bank of Zanzibar), in 1977 I stood for election for the South Region constituency, and was elected MP for South Region of Pemba.

A good leader must understand the need for continued growth in his or her life, because it is a constant striving for growth and improvement that will take you and your organisation to another level. Learn to respect and win people over, instead of using power to bend people to your will.

The attitude to public services changed during my time in a ministerial position because I was ready to learn, to listen and make collective decisions. Honesty is the key to Public Service. My greatest duty is to make sure I supervise and enforce if necessary the implementation of our decisions. It is through this and the power of persuasion that I am fortunate to enjoy the confidence and good working relationship with those we are elected to serve. I have always tried to keep some words of Gandhi at the forefront of my mind: "An ounce of practice is worth more than tons of preaching".

3) In what ways do you believe that being a Minister is somewhat akin to tightrope walking?

Being a minister means you are a public figure, you have no privacy, and people expect you to deliver although sometimes you may wish to do things your own way, but constitutional and political constraints provide real challenges, ones which can frustrate you or make you feel what you are doing is akin to tightrope walking. You need to persevere and work constructively with different groups, especially in government to find the best solution to problems.

Just to share with you one example, in 1983 after visiting various prisons across Tanzania I discovered that prisoners were not getting sufficient nutrition. Whilst we had sufficient manpower, land etc. the Government had very little money for prisoners' meals and they were weak and many were falling ill. The Government has a duty of care to all its citizens, even those who have transgressed. I went to the President to raise my concerns and he asked me what I believed the solution was. I suggested two options, one to release certain detainees that were not a threat to society and had served the bulk of their sentence and secondly to provide certain means to help produce more fresh produce. Luckily, he agreed to both options and for the second one he asked me to present my ideas to the Cabinet as it passed the budget. I requested the Cabinet to approve my plan for prison inmates to be allowed to grow produce, enough for their own consumption and if there was an excess this could be sold in the markets. In order to do this I needed 100 tractors, as well as agricultural equipment and seeds for 6 months to initiate the programme and I said that if I was not able to implement the programme I was ready to resign.

Through persuasion, honesty and commitment my budget was approved. I made something of a name for myself. We achieved all our goals, detainees were released after scrutiny and a commitment from them to write to the President asking him for an amnesty. I kept my word and the Prison Department from that time until I left the office in 1987 was self-sufficient in fresh produce, sugar, soap and a range of other products.

4) What has been the greatest challenge that you have faced since becoming a Minister?

The greatest challenges facing third world ministers are budget deficits, corruption and mismanagement of limited resources. Being honest and committed to achieve my objectives which are within the government plans I had to be creative, innovative and have a sound understanding that we have budgetary constraints. I have always endeavoured to rise to this challenge, and this is why I had to use a practical approach to solving complicated issues like food shortages in prison, the overcrowding of inmates, tackling crime, provision of housing etc. In seeking to tackle these pressing issues I managed to reduce some of these problems by persuading good friends of Tanzania to assist in some capacity. The German Government donated 20 cars for patrols, DPRK (North Korea) assisted in agriculture, housing and sports fields, and China gave us essential fire fighting equipment etc.

5) As an experienced Minister what advice would you give to a new minister upon taking office?

All of us when we take office take an oath, first you have to believe in it, that you are not contracting yourself with the Executive only, but with the Almighty God too and people will make you accountable for that.

Secondly, one has to realise that the position was not created for him alone, and he is just lucky to be given that opportunity to administer that office. He has to be honest, committed and down to the earth, patient with family members and with others.

Thirdly, respect of the Law is key to achieving your objectives, and the constitution, laws and standing orders are key instruments to help you to perform any ministerial duties.

Fourthly, he has to extremely good in building relationships with the parliamentarians, standing committee members and his staff in the ministry, not to forget he has been elected, hence his constituency should be a model for performing his duties.

Fifthly, he should not commit himself to anything over which he has no control.

He should do his or her best to deliver justice to all, and avoid all forms of discrimination—religious, tribal, gender bias etc.

Be positive in all things.

6) Are you aware of any training or induction offered to Ministers? If so what form does this take and how has it helped Ministers to carry out their role?

When I began my political career our Party had an Ideological College that used to provide training to our leaders at different levels. Some also used to be trained at our Army Institute, so even if you were not nominated to a ministerial position at least you were given some key leadership skills. Also I remember on my first appointment, the then President chaired a seminar with his ministers and we were given general guidelines about our responsibilities. Even today the President has been doing the same thing.

But this is not enough, because the environment has changed - the world is becoming smaller and smaller, and technology is changing rapidly. Continuous training regarding the Rule of Law, human rights issues, Parliamentary diplomacy, climate change, negotiations, conflict resolution and its aftermath, budget cycles, donor funding, how the world's financial organisations operate and the roll of the private sector in our economies (PPP, BOT etc.) e-government and e-procurement are very fundamental topics. The results of training can be patchy, but overall I believe that it is extremely important and more is needed.

7) There is often much talk of the Corridors of Power but precious little talk of the Corridors of Responsibility. How can we ensure that Ministers internationally have a greater appreciation of the importance of responsibility?

The minister has responsibility for policy issues, resources, interdepartmental coordination and intentional relations with its counterpart ministries in countries where there exist bilateral relations.

The minister's central role is to advise the President and Prime Minister and provide him or her with the broadest possible expert support in all of the minister's responsibilities.

The minister oversees issues affecting his or her country internationally e.g. bilateral trade, climate change etc and engagement with organisations such as UN, AU, EU etc.

About the Authors

Aliar Hossain

Aliar Hossain was born in Bangladesh in Narayanganj, a city known as the Dandy of the East. He is the youngest son of the late Ali Hossain and comes from a family with a deep commitment to community, religion, politics, and business (i.e., family owned or managed local mosque, charitable dispensary, medical services, and education institutions). Aliar was strongly influenced by a commitment to continuing his family's traditions from his childhood.

Aliar's mission is to raise public awareness for the fair politics and governance, fight against corruption, the concept of global citizenship, importance of doing business ethically, and the significance of sustainable development in the global village. He is currently undertaking PhD research with Cardiff School of Management. He is also acting as MBA supervisor and visiting lecturer for a number of UK business schools. He has visited numerous UK and Asian universities and colleges as speaker for change management, CSR, leadership development, corporate culture, globalization, and sustainable development issues.

His first book was published in 2011 (Sustainable Development Handbook: A South Asian Perspective). Some other published papers include "Changing Markets: The Future for Higher Education in a Globalised World" (LSBM, 2012), "Strategic and Pragmatic E-Business"

(IGI Global, 2012), "Impact of Micro Finance" (Digibiz, 2009), "Information Security and Threats: E-Commerce Banking" (both International Conference on Security and Management, USA, 2009).

He has also professional and academic membership with a number of organizations both in the UK and abroad (Institute of Consulting, Regents Business Forum, Royal Institute of International Affairs, International Journal of Contemporary Research in Management and Social Sciences, and many more).

He is the founder and director of Regents Consulting Services Ltd., which works to enable corporate social responsibility, political training, and sustainable development through consultation and improved management strategies, involving corporate and executive training and visits to business schools in the UK and abroad. Aliar funds and manages Seed of Possibilities, a social and economic development not-for-profit project providing grants and consultation for poor people in the South Asian region, improving their living standards with sustainable business ideas, funding and long-term professional support.

Mark T. Jones

Mark is a fervent internationalist who is widely traveled. In the year 2000, he initiated and oversaw a major humanitarian venture into war-torn Sierra Leone and then spent two years in the Middle East where he worked in Jordan (2002–2004). An orator of distinction, he is the author of several books and numerous articles and in 2009 produced a forward strategy for the sericulture sector in Bangladesh entitled Rajshahi: the Silk Sensation. Mark trains legislative leaders and is an adviser on trade and investment in Africa's frontier markets. Mark believes that many of the current economic and geopolitical difficulties in the world are the result of a combination of a poverty of leadership, poor regional/market knowledge, and a lack of strategic vision.